PRO FOOTBALL'S TEN GREATEST GAMES

ALSO BY JOHN THORN

Baseball's Ten Greatest Games
The Relief Pitcher
A Century of Baseball Lore

PRO FOOTBALL'S TEN GREATEST GAMES

BY JOHN THORN

Foreword by Terry Bradshaw

FOUR WINDS PRESS, NEW YORK

PHOTO CREDITS

Akron Beacon Journal, 38-39; Vernon J. Biever, 108; Chicago Bears, 10; Dallas Cowboys, 180; Miami Dolphins, 162; New Orleans Saints, 154-55; New York Jets, 121; Pro Football Hall of Fame, 17, 20-21, 34-35, 46, 54, 65, 91; United Press International, 12-13, 49, 72-73, 77, 85, 98, 104-105, 130, 134-35, 141, 165, 172-73, 182-83, 194-95; Wide World Photos, 29, 60-61, 117.

LIBRARY OF CONGRESS CATALOGING IN PUBLICATION DATA

Thorn, John (date)
   Pro football's ten greatest games.

   Includes index.
   1. Football. 2. Professional sports—United States.
I. Title.
GV954.T47   796.332′64′0973   81-65909
ISBN 0-590-07788-0   AACR2

Published by Four Winds Press
A division of Scholastic Inc.
Copyright © 1981 by John Thorn
All rights reserved
Printed in the United States of America
Library of Congress Catalog Card Number: 81-65909
Book design by Constance Ftera
1 2 3 4 5   85 84 83 82 81

For Eric and Melissa

ACKNOWLEDGMENTS

For help in tracking down the countless small details which bring my ten games to life, I thank:

The men who played in these games and who, even as much as half a century later, recalled the events to me as clearly as if the games had been played yesterday.

The Pro Football Hall of Fame, in particular its curator-researcher Joe Horrigan, who was exceedingly cooperative and helpful.

The staffs of the public libraries whose research facilities I used, namely those of New York, Chicago, Cleveland, and Saugerties, my home town.

The public-relations directors of the NFL clubs which were involved in these ten games, particularly Ted Haracz of the Bears and Ed Croke of the Giants.

The National Football League, with special thanks to AFC Director of Information Joe Browne and NFC Public Relations Assistant Pete Abitante.

Jon Landman, who provided vital assistance with some murky aspects of the 1933 game.

And for other sorts of help along the way, thanks to:

David Reuther, my editor and friend.

Susan Albury, who skillfully guided this book through its stages of production.

Joan Raines, my esteemed agent and advisor.

And, of course, my two sons and my wife, none of them sports fans, who amiably indulge me.

CONTENTS

FOREWORD

Pro football is not an easy game to play. It's not an easy game to watch, either—if a quarterback can't read a rotating zone defense, Lord help the poor spectator. And it's not an easy game to write about, because so much of the key action takes place within the line, hidden from view; or away from the ball, where decoys can clear the way for a long gainer.

Yet America is crazy about pro football. Why? For the very thing that makes it "difficult"—it is a *team* game like no other. Baseball is first and foremost a confrontation between pitcher and batter; a Sandy Koufax can make up for all kinds of deficiencies in team play. A basketball superstar can take control of the ball and convert a five-on-five game into a one-on-one shootout. But in football, the snap propels twenty-two men in motion simultaneously, each with an assigned role that is absolutely crucial to the outcome of the play. A would-be hotshot at one of the "glamor" positions (quarterback, running back, wide receiver) will be whittled down to size right quick if his teammates don't execute their responsibilities.

Give a runner a hole, give a passer time, and more often than not he will succeed. Force the man with the ball to improvise behind the line, to seek yardage on his own, and more often than not he will fail.

In a sense, there are *no* individual accomplishments at all in football, nothing like a home run or a long jumpshot. My most memorable "individual" accomplishment as a pro came in the 1979 Super Bowl, when the Steelers defeated the Cowboys by a score of 35-31. I passed for a record four touchdowns and 318 yards, and was named the game's Most Valuable Player. But whatever glory attached itself to that performance belonged no more to me than to the other members of the offensive unit, and that's not humble pie—it's just common sense, what every football player knows. I didn't do it alone; no quarterback ever has. And the satisfaction of that Super Bowl passing record was far outweighed by the joy of victory in which the whole Pittsburgh organization shared.

That feeling of shared accomplishment can be found in any winning football locker room. It's the part of the game that I will miss most when my playing days are behind me.

Pro Football's Ten Greatest Games captures that sense of *teamness,* of unified purpose, which is unique to the sport. Most football writers focus on "key" plays and players, magnifying their importance and diminishing other facets; they miss the true flow of the game. John Thorn catches it and pins it to the page. Reading about these ten fabulous contests is even better than being there—it's like viewing the game films with the coach at your side. I loved the book, and I know you will, too.

TERRY BRADSHAW

PRO FOOTBALL'S TEN GREATEST GAMES

INTRODUCTION

What's the greatest football game you ever saw? Was it a bombs-away affair, with the outcome in doubt until the final gun? Or a defensive standoff, a taut tug-of-war in which the punts were many and the points few? Purists will prefer the low-scoring battle in the trenches, for line play is the essence of the game, the aspect that links football with ancient combat and distinguishes it from, say, basketball. Yet most fans find their attentions wandering in a contest that bangs and smashes its way to a 6–3 conclusion; they like to see an occasional touchdown. Nonstop offense (Oakland once defeated Houston 52–49!) may be sloppy, sandlot stuff unworthy of professionals, but nonstop defense, no matter how artful or bruising, does not make for great football either.

In fact, it was the excellence of defensive play that nearly killed the National Football League half a century ago. To tell the story of pro football's crisis and its odd rescue, however, I should step back a few years earlier still, to the origin of the NFL.

The American Professional Football Association was born in 1920 over a few buckets of beer in a Hupmobile auto showroom in Canton, Ohio. For the next few seasons, while college

1

football was booming, the APFA—rechristened as the National Football League—flirted with extinction: it shuffled franchises and playing dates in dizzying fashion while struggling to convince the public that its performers blocked clean, tackled hard, and truly cared about winning.

Then, in 1925, college hero Red Grange signed with the Chicago Bears and jolted the NFL into instant respectability and profitability. The "Galloping Ghost" was filling stadiums from New York to Los Angeles; and though folks came to see Grange, they stayed to see professional football. Grange himself thought prospects for the pros so promising that he left the Bears in 1926 to spearhead a new American Football League. Alas, the golden era was over just as it seemed to be dawning. The AFL crashed after one disastrous season, taking twelve of the twenty-two NFL clubs with it.

The pared-down league fared reasonably well through the rest of the decade. But the Great Depression intensified the competition between colleges and pros for the public's dollar, and once again interest in the league began to drop off dangerously. In 1930 the NFL lost one franchise; in 1931, another; in 1932, two more. Dull offensive strategy, low scores, and frequent ties were souring even the diehard fans. In 1932 the NFL's leading passer completed not even three passes per game, and five teams scored under 8 points per game. The season ended in a deadlock for the championship between the Bears, with a record of six wins, one loss, and *six ties*, and the Portsmouth Spartans, who also finished six and one, but with four ties. Neither team had averaged as many as 12 points. The pro game was dying, and this time no college boy stood poised to pull it back from the brink.

In the week leading up to the December 18 playoff for the title, a snowstorm hit Chicago and temperatures reached thirty degrees below zero. Bears' owner George Halas, deep in the red despite his share of the championship, realized that if the game were to be held at Wrigley Field as planned, more people might be playing it than watching it. He moved the game indoors to the Chicago Stadium and attracted 11,198 curious spectators, a fine crowd by that year's standards.

Playing conditions were bizarre. The aromatic turf on which the teams clashed had been dumped on the concrete floor by a recently departed circus. The field was twenty yards too short and ten yards too narrow, and was enclosed by a five-foot-high fence. Because of the cramped quarters, the goalposts were only a hundred yards apart rather than the required one hundred twenty, and the two teams agreed to bring the ball in ten yards whenever the previous play had been downed within five yards of the sideline.

These inventions born of necessity seemed to open up the game; both teams moved the ball and presented numerous scoring threats. However, all these fizzled inside the 20-yard line, and neither team took advantage of the drawn-in goalposts to attempt a three-pointer. Through three quarters the game was scoreless. At last, late in the fourth period the Bears' Dick Nesbitt intercepted a pass and returned it to the Portsmouth 7. Fullback Bronko Nagurski drove to the 2 on first down, but was stopped short of the goal on his next two plunges. On fourth down, he grabbed the handoff and took one deliberate step toward the line, then faded back a few feet and lobbed a pass into the arms of Red Grange, unguarded in the end zone. The Spartans' coach, Potsy Clark, protested strenuously that Nagurski had not dropped back the mandated five yards before unloading the ball—but the points were on the scoreboard, and this was, after all, Chicago and not Portsmouth. A last-minute safety made the final score 9–0.

The "five yards back" rule had been authored by the intercollegiate rules committee, as was virtually the entire NFL rulebook. Together with the watermelon shape of the pigskin, this rule severely shackled the aerial game that the public longed to see. In the league's winter meetings prior to the 1933 season, rookie Boston Redskin owner George Preston Marshall combined forces with the Bears' Halas, who had been present at the creation of the NFL, to improve their product. Both had lost a bundle in '32, and their vision was clear enough to see the writing on the wall. They shoved through new rules which made permanent the temporary measures that had streamlined the indoor championship—including the officials' charitable view of the Nagurski pass. Moving the goalposts up ten yards, from the back of the end zone to the goal line, would make the field goal a vital offensive weapon again after several years on the shelf. Employing hashmarks set in ten yards from the sidelines would permit the offense to use more of the field and not be compelled to waste a down just to bring the ball back toward the center of the playing area. And by allowing a passer the freedom to release the ball from any point behind the line of scrimmage, the NFL would now offer America a game more deceptive, more swift, and more explosive than the one being played on the campuses.

To top off these innovations, Marshall also prompted the league to split its teams into two divisions, with the divisional titlists to meet in the first scheduled postseason championship game. The following year, 1934, would produce the slimmed-down modern ball.

At its darkest hour pro football looked forward (with a glance back to its indoor playoff match for inspiration) and recreated itself. The game as we know it today—a sleek, complex blend of strength and style that captivates millions—can be envisioned on the playing fields of 1933. And that's where our journey through time, reliving the ten greatest pro football games ever played, is about to begin. Won't you come along?

JOHN THORN
Saugerties, New York

December 17, 1933

NEW YORK GIANTS

VS.

CHICAGO BEARS

A raw, wet wind blows in from the east, and mist and fog hang over Wrigley Field. Kickoff for this first NFL championship is at 1:45, only a few minutes away.

As we take our seats on the 50-yard line, the eighteen men of each team race onto the field to a roar of anticipation. The match figures to be a beaut, for both the Giants and Bears coasted to their divisional titles and split two hard-fought regular-season meetings. New York's single-wing offense, led by the passing of tailback Harry Newman and the running of fullback Ken Strong, is the sensation of the league, having piled up a record number of points. The Bears, on the other hand, boast the NFL's second-stingiest defense along with a T-formation attack in which fullback Bronko Nagurski supplies the power

5

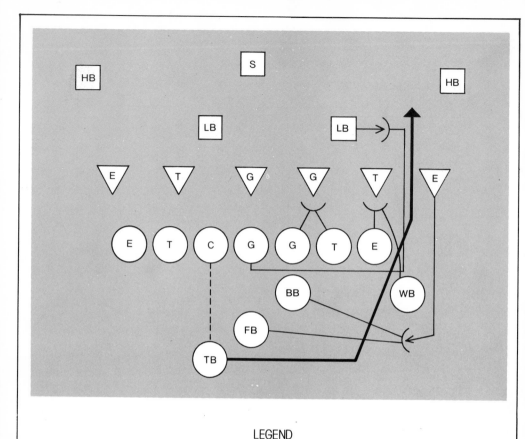

LEGEND

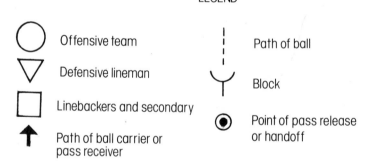

○ Offensive team

▽ Defensive lineman

☐ Linebackers and secondary

↑ Path of ball carrier or pass receiver

╎ Path of ball

⌣ Block

◉ Point of pass release or handoff

The single-wing formation takes its name from the positioning of a halfback on the "wing" just outside the strong-side end. In the off-tackle play above, the ball is snapped to the tailback, standing five yards behind the center. The wingback and end push the defensive tackle to the inside, while the fullback and blocking back seal the defensive end to the outside. The running guard leads the tailback through the resulting hole and blocks the linebacker.

and everyone is a threat to pass. The football will be flying today, I assure you, in a razzle-dazzle display rarely if ever equaled since.

In the week before the championship, Giants' coach Steve Owen readied his troops for every known variation in the Bears' whirling T. He still burns over the midseason loss in which Chicago end Bill Hewitt threw a pass off an end-around for the winning score. And in the "skull drill" meeting last night Ray Flaherty, who is the team's right end, captain, and assistant coach, drew particular attention to the fake-plunge and jump-pass with which Nagurski won last year's title.

Now the teams line up for the kickoff, the Giants to receive. The ball sails into the arms of Newman, who returns to the 30. The dark-jerseyed, leather-helmeted Giants line up in the single wing, the form of attack employed by every NFL club this year except the Bears. An unbalanced formation—with both guards on the same side of the center—it is founded on power blocking rather than on the deception of the T. The single wing is designed to pit two blockers against each key defender on football's basic play, the off-tackle run to the strong side (see diagram).

Essential to the success of the single wing is a tailback who is a triple threat. Harry Newman, a rookie All-American from Michigan, is that and more: he is the league's top passer; leads his team in rushing; returns kickoffs and punts; plays defensive halfback; and chips in with an occasional field goal, extra point, or quick kick. Joining Harry in the backfield are fullback Ken Strong, who joined the Giants this year when the Staten Island Stapletons folded; wingback Dale Burnett, the club's speed merchant and best receiver; and blocking back Bo Molenda, a bruiser who weighs nearly as much as the interior linemen. At the ends are two-time all-pros Red Badgro and Ray Flaherty. And in the trenches, where football's most important players toil in obscurity, are tackles Len Grant and Bill Owen (the coach's brother), guards Potsy Jones and Butch Gibson (faster than many backs), and center Mel Hein (simply the best there is).

Now for some high-powered offense, right? Hardly. The Giants run three times and punt. The Bears do the same. Another cautious possession follows for each team—not a pass thrown, not a first down gained. This is caveman football. When will we see the promised fireworks, you ask?

Soon, soon. For the time being, coaches Halas and Owen are content to feel each other out. Like two boxers in the early rounds of a long fight, neither wants to create the first opening with a mistake. Despite this year's liberalized passing rule, pro football is still learning how to put the ball in the air and interceptions are frequent. It still borders on heresy to throw the ball inside your own 40-yard line. So teams will run and punt, run and punt—often kicking away on early downs—until a break comes along.

At last it does. Keith Molesworth, the Bears' diminutive halfback, lofts a punt to Newman, who finds a crack straight up the center and scoots some twenty yards to midfield. On first down Strong sweeps left for six before being run out of bounds. Now Newman fields the snap and readies to arch his first pass, to Burnett over the middle—but the ball is batted away at the line of scrimmage. (Harry stands only five feet eight inches, not an ideal height for a passer.) Third down, four yards to go, with the ball still at the left hashmark.

The Giants line up unbalanced to the right, with left tackle Grant standing to the right of center Hein. Now comes a surprise the Giants have cooked up especially for this game: In a simultaneous shift, left end Badgro pulls back from the line, wingback Burnett steps up alongside Flaherty, and Newman moves in behind center, just as a T quarterback would. Thus Burnett has become the right end, Flaherty is no longer an eligible receiver, Badgro is a back, and the left end is . . . Hein! Mel snaps to Newman, who drops the ball back into Mel's hands before spinning and "tripping." George Musso, the Bears' behemoth tackle, pounces on the fallen tailback and actually shakes him, looking for the ball. Meanwhile, Hein fakes a block and strolls downfield, concealing the ball and waiting for his interference to form. But after walking ten yards unnoticed, Mel becomes excited and hightails it up the sideline. All that stands between him and end-zone glory is Molesworth, the last man back in the Bears' 6-2-2-1 defense, who is about to be cleared out by Badgro and Burnett. But Hein's haste arouses Moley's suspicions; the safety dashes off in pursuit before the Giant blockers can converge on him. Having the angle on Hein, he fences him in at the 15-yard line.

This center-eligible play, coined the Hein Special, has given the Giants the game's first scoring threat, but they do not capitalize. On fourth down they scorn the easy field goal and are stopped at the 7. The Bears take over, but Owen doesn't mind too much; indeed, his game plan is to keep the Bears bottled in their own territory, where their laterals and reverses and halfback options are taboo.

But Chicago plays hot-potato with the ball immediately. On first down quarterback Carl Brumbaugh flips back to Molesworth, who quick-kicks over the head of safety Newman, who had been playing only twenty yards off the line. The pigskin hits at the Chicago 45, then takes a huge Bear bounce. Ken Strong races back into Giant territory to retrieve the ball, but is dragged down at his own 42.

On first down, Newman tries to keep up the pressure. He passes over the middle for Flaherty, but the throw is behind him. Linebacker Nagurski plucks it out of the air easily and charges to the New York 26, where he is finally hauled down by five Giants. Now the Bears can play all of their cards.

The backfield consists of: Brumbaugh, the team's quarterback

Bronko Nagurski

since 1930, when the Bears added the man-in-motion to football's oldest formation; Molesworth, the left halfback who generally throws more often than Brumbaugh; right halfback Gene Ronzani, a quarterback in college who also wings the ball quite a bit but is prized for his blocking; and the incomparable Nagurski, a 238-pound fullback who tramples would-be tacklers with his head down, his torso nearly horizontal to the ground, and his knees pumping. Before today's game, coach Owen assigned two men to cover this human locomotive on every play and instructed the Giants to throw themselves at his legs in hopes of tripping him rather than risk life and limb by tackling him head-on. At the ends are Bill Karr, a rookie from West Virginia who became a starter in midseason when Luke Johnsos broke an ankle, and Bill Hewitt, an all-pro from Michigan (where his quarterback was Newman) who can be spotted easily because he wears no helmet. At the tackles are George "Moose" Musso, a 270-pound freshman, and Link Lyman, a thirty-five-year-old veteran who revolutionized defensive line play in the twenties by shifting his position before the snap. The guards are Zuck Carlson and Joe Kopcha, each an all-pro, and the center is Ookie Miller, who plays linebacker along with Nagurski.

On first down Brumbaugh hands to Ronzani, who busts off right tackle for eleven. But the next three plays yield only eight yards, and on fourth and two Halas brings in "Automatic Jack"

Manders to attempt a field goal. He splits the uprights and the Bears lead 3–0. Where Owen had opted for defensive field position, Halas went for the points. They will matter.

Following the kickoff, the Giants are stymied inside their 25. On third down reserve halfback Kink Richards, in for Strong, attempts a quick kick. Bill Hewitt rushes in to block it, but fortunately for New York, Burnett recovers. Now, on fourth down, Richards drops back and gets the boot away. The veteran Red Grange, in the game for Brumbaugh, takes the line-drive kick at his own 30 and navigates skillfully to the New York 46. Since Grange wrecked his knee in 1927, he has been "just another straight runner," he acknowledges, "and the woods are filled with straight runners." But Number 77 is still a threat on offense, and one of his generation's great defensive backs.

The first quarter ends on that punt return, and the Bears open the second with Molesworth at quarterback, Grange and Ronzani at the halves, and Manders at fullback. On first down Ronzani takes the handoff from Molesworth, then flips the ball over the line to him. Moley makes a marvelous grab and carries down to the 29. Repeating the play but this time keeping the ball, Ronzani picks up two; but then a couple of incomplete passes and an offside penalty move the Bears back to the 32. Halas calls for a field-goal attempt from the 40, a prodigious blast in these days, and Manders complies, knocking it over the crossbar with several yards to spare.

The score is only 6–0. Still, you can't help feeling that the game is slowly slipping away from the Giants. Their running game has gone nowhere, and their only pass completion has been the trick play, in which the ball traveled perhaps six inches in the air. After Flaherty returns Manders's squib kickoff to the 38, the Giants continue in their inept ways, to the delight of the crowd. Newman overthrows Flaherty on first down, and his next toss is batted down by Lyman. Luckily, an overzealous Musso anticipated the snap and charged offside. With a second and five, Newman can call for a run or a pass; he slips the ball

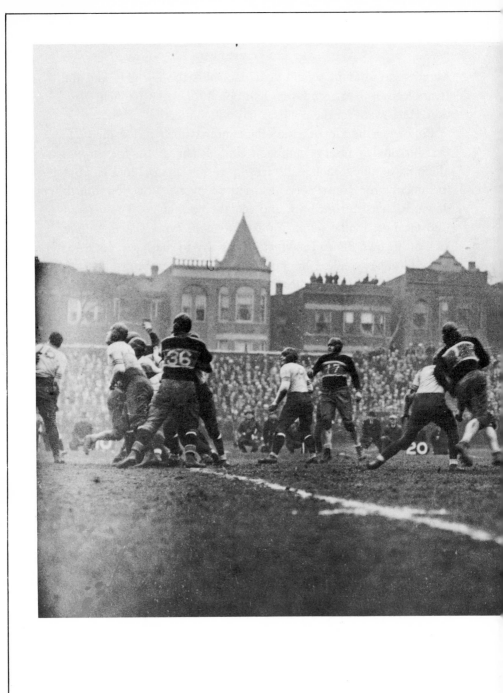

In third-period action, Jack Manders attempts a field goal from the 18-yard line; the holder is Carl Brumbaugh. Following Nagurski as the University of Minnesota fullback, Manders won All-American honors last year, as did Harry Newman of the Giants.

to Kink Richards on a counter play off left tackle. Richards, an unheralded swifty from little Simpson College, weaves his way through the Bears' secondary for a twenty-eight-yard gain.

Heartened by this first productive conventional play, Newman goes back to the air. He spots Red Badgro ten yards downfield, with a full stride on the defender. Badgro catches the ball in motion and gallops to the end zone untouched. Strong adds the point, and suddenly the Giants lead 7–6.

What a turnabout! The stadium is deathly still, and the Bears scarcely know what hit them. They run through their plays in a daze, and for the next few series the game reverts to a punting duel. In the final minutes of the half, however, Nagurski and Ronzani pound the Giant line for several solid gains which produce three first downs. With the ball on the Giant 26 and seconds to play, Grange sweeps left end for seventeen yards but does not manage to get out of bounds. Chicago has consumed all of its timeouts, and as the crowd buzzes nervously, the Bears hurriedly assemble in field-goal formation. Manders gets the kick off as time runs out—but his sharply angled seventeen-yard attempt sails wide to the right.

The first half has been tense and well played, but certainly no barn-burner. The Bears outgained the Giants by a wide margin, especially on the ground, yet walked off the field on the short end of the score. At intermission, coach Halas will labor mightily to combat his team's sense of frustration. It is critical that the Bears, with the opening possession of the second half, retake control of the game.

George Corbett, a chunky little back from Millikin University, brings the second-half kickoff back to the 24. Nagurski rips off runs of fourteen and seven yards, knocking defenders down like bowling pins. After an incomplete pass, Ronzani bursts through the Giant line, suddenly made of cheesecloth, for fifteen. Now Brumbaugh takes the snap and hands to Corbett, who circles left while the quarterback slips over the line. Corbett pulls up and lobs a little pass to Brummy, who makes it all the way down to the 13. The Bears have moved upfield almost at will; but here, in the shadow of their own goalposts, the Giants stiffen their resolve. The next three plays net only three yards, and the Bears must settle for Manders's third field goal of the day. (During the entire regular season he knocked home five—and that led the league!)

Fielding the kickoff on the 5, Newman returns to the 27. With the Bears' linebackers positioned tightly behind the line in expectation of a run, Newman rolls to the right and fires to Burnett for twenty-three yards. The play worked so well that Harry calls it again, and this time it clicks for thirteen. Now comes a bullet over the middle to Richards, good for fifteen. The Bears' backs are like ducks in a shooting gallery, being picked off no matter which way they turn. With the ball on the Chicago 22, Newman rolls left behind Grant and Gibson but stops just short of the scrimmage line. He shovels a pass to Badgro, who takes it upfield to the 9. An illegal-motion penalty and an incompletion stall the Giants momentarily; but from the 14 Newman connects with reserve blocking back Max Krause on a sideline pass down to the 1. Richards's thrust up the middle is stopped for no gain, then Krause burrows under his blockers for the score. Strong tacks on the point and the Giants are back on top, 14–9. We have seen five scoring plays already, more than most entire games provided this year.

Strong kicks off to Corbett, who only gets as far as the 23. The Bears try to better their field position on the ground, but Corbett is stopped for no gain and Nagurski picks up a mere two. Rather than chance an interception on third and long, Molesworth drops back in punt formation. But instead of punting, he shot-puts the ball to midfield, where Corbett runs under it. Twisting and dodging, breaking tackle after tackle, little George weaves his way downfield—then laterals to Bill Karr, who goes all the way to the New York 8, a gain of sixty-seven yards!

Two rushes by Molesworth bring the ball to the 6 as the Giants once again try to bend without breaking. On third and goal, Nagurski drives toward the center of the line, then stops, jumps, and fires to Bill Karr for the touchdown. Despite Flaherty's warnings last night, no Giant is within five yards of Karr. Manders's point-after puts Chicago back on top for the third time, 16–14.

Strong lugs the kickoff back to the 24, and Newman picks up where he left off. Throwing caution to the winds, he hits Flaherty for eleven, Burnett for eighteen, and Badgro for eleven. With the Bears back on their heels, trying to figure out where the next dart will land, Newman sends Strong up the middle for fourteen. From the Chicago 22, he again finds Burnett at the right sideline, and Dale spins upfield to the 8 as the gun sounds ending the third quarter. In this period alone, Newman has completed nine of ten passes for 131 yards. To appreciate the magnitude of this aerial display, consider that for the entire season, fourteen games, Newman passed for only sixty-nine yards per contest—and established a new pro record at that!

On the first play of the final period, with the ball spotted at the right hashmark, the Giants line up unbalanced to the right, a formation which seems to indicate either a pass or an inside run. Yet, at the snap, Strong loops behind Newman, takes a short pitch, and motors toward the left end. The play is slow to develop, however, and the right side of the Bear line closes off the outside. About to swallow a loss, Strong heaves an overhand lateral back across the field. The ball flutters over to Newman like a dying quail, for Strong can scarcely close his hand on the football to throw it: a few years back, he injured his right wrist playing baseball and the doctor who operated on him removed the wrong bone, thus ending his prospective career with the Detroit Tigers.

Newman juggles the ball, then scrambles right, dodging tack-

New York owner Tim Mara signed Michigan star Harry Newman specifically to take advantage of the NFL's new passing rule. Newman has the knack of rolling out, stopping short, and firing a bullet downfield—no mean feat with the watermelon ball of 1933.

lers while giving up ground to the 15. As the entire Bear team focuses its energies on corralling Newman, Strong drifts unaccompanied into the left portion of the end zone and waves for the ball. Newman heaves it nearly fifty yards across the field. Strong runs to the corner, snares the pass, then stumbles out of bounds. This sandlot hocus-pocus is pure inspiration, though in later years it will find its way into the Giants' playbook (it will never work again). Strong provides the extra point, and the Giants go ahead 21–16. The fans can scarcely believe what they are seeing.

In the first half we wondered when we would see some offense; now the question is when we will see some defense. Will the last team to have the ball be the winner?

After the kickoff, the Bears move briskly from the 28 to their 45, all but three of the yards provided by Nagurski thrusts. Then on three disastrous wide runs by Molesworth, Corbett, and Ronzani, the Bears lose a whopping twenty-five yards and are forced to punt.

Now, with most of the final period left to play, the Giants turn conservative in an effort to protect their lead. They rush the ball routinely three times and punt, then their defense holds the Bears to a lone first down. Once again, the Giants eat up the clock with three rushes, but this time Strong's kick is low— Molesworth grabs it on the run and scoots to the New York 48. This looks to be a great opportunity, but on third down and one, Ronzani's surprise pass is picked off by linebacker Max Krause and returned to the Giant 34.

Owen isn't going to let Newman throw the ball this late in the game, so the Bears brace for the run. Three ground plays net a mere four yards, and once again Strong drops into deep punt formation. In the face of a mighty rush from ends Hewitt and Karr, Ken shanks the kick out of bounds at his own 46—a mere eight yards from scrimmage. Can New York's defense hold again?

Brumbaugh returns to the game in place of Corbett, and on first down takes a pass from Molesworth for nine. On second down Nagurski bulls his way up the middle for four, putting the ball on the 33. Less than two minutes remain to be played. Grange, a superior blocker, comes in for Molesworth. Brumbaugh lines up not under the center, Ookie Miller, but behind right guard Zuck Carlson. He takes the snap, fakes a handoff to Red, then slaps the ball into Nagurski's belly. Bronko lowers his head, aiming for the middle again, but instead of proceeding through the hole, he straightens up, leaps, and lobs the ball to Hewitt some ten yards downfield. Hewitt takes two steps, with Burnett on his heels. But before Hewitt can be thrown down, he laterals to Karr, who races toward the right corner chased by Strong and Newman. One or the other should nail him at about the 8—but out of nowhere comes Ronzani to throw himself in front of the two Giants and knock them both "right on their cans," as he will say after the game. Karr trots into the end zone as the fans yell themselves silly. The Bears lead 22–21. Halas lets Ronzani try the meaningless PAT. Gene boots it through, and the Bears prepare to defend their lead for the final minute.

The Giants have made a classic mistake, one that will be repeated as long as football is played—they packed up their offense before the final minutes. Trying to sit on a scant lead, they thought time was their ally; now it is most certainly their foe.

They get an unforeseen break: Strong returns the kickoff straight up the middle to the 40, nearly breaking away for the distance. Now the Giants need only twenty-five yards to move within range of Strong's powerful right leg. They must rev up their passing game once more, if they haven't forgotten how.

Less than a minute remains to be played. Everyone in the park is on his feet. Newman lines his men up, then calls for a shift to the center-eligible play which bedeviled the Bears in the first period. He takes the snap, whirls—but this time he does not

This is one of pro football's classic photographs. The helmetless Bill Hewitt, in the clutches of New York's Dale Burnett, flips a lateral. Bill Karr is about to grab it and race for the end zone.

return the ball to Hein, instead pitching back to Burnett, who has the strongest arm on the field. Once the ball is pitched out where all can see it, Hein, incredibly enough, is allowed to drift downfield to the Chicago 30. Burnett rears back to fire the long pass across the field but is hit just at the moment of release. The pass wobbles toward Hein, seeming to take forever to reach him. Brumbaugh, nowhere near Hein as Burnett cocked his arm, has time to race over from his safety position and tip the pass away.

Time now for just one more desperation play. Returning to the single wing, Newman fakes to Strong while Badgro and Flaherty run patterns to the left side of the field. Then he flips a little pass off to the right to Burnett, who runs straight at Grange, playing some twenty yards off the line of scrimmage in a 1930s version of the "prevent" defense. Jogging undefended alongside Burnett is Hein, ready to receive a lateral the moment Grange makes a move for Burnett. But Red looks in Burnett's eyes, senses his own dilemma and, with the instincts of a truly exceptional player, makes what George Halas in years to come will describe as "the greatest defensive play I ever saw": He tackles Burnett around the chest, pinning his arms so he cannot flip the ball to Hein. Grange doesn't even try to bring Burnett down; he is content to lock him in a bearhug as Hein pleads for the ball and time runs out.

The conclusion leaves us gasping. This game has had it all—laterals, reverses, flea-flickers, fake punts; bull's-eye passing, power running, deadly kicking; stratagem and counterstratagem. The Bears have won the first NFL championship game, but the real victor is the league itself, which has shown the nation the brand of ball the pros can play. The college coaches will call it basketball to disparage its aerial options, but soon they will imitate it. The future of football has been glimpsed today.

SCORING

GIANTS	0	7	7	7 — 21
BEARS	3	3	10	7 — 23

Chi.: Manders, FG, 15.
Chi.: Manders, FG, 40.
N.Y.: Badgro, 29, pass from Newman (Strong, kick).
Chi.: Manders, FG, 18.
N.Y.: Krause, 1, run (Strong, kick).
Chi.: Karr, 6, pass from Nagurski (Manders, kick).
N.Y.: Strong, 8, pass from Newman (Strong, kick).
Chi.: Karr, 33, lateral from Hewitt after pass from Nagurski (Ronzani, kick).

TEAM STATISTICS

	Giants	Bears
First downs	13	13
Rushing yardage	80	165
Passing yardage	201	160
Punt return yardage	59	58
Passes	13-19	7-16
Interceptions by	1	1
Punts	14-31	10-42
Fumbles lost	0	0
Yards penalized	15	35

(Authoritative individual statistics not available)

December 24, 1950

LOS ANGELES RAMS

VS.

CLEVELAND BROWNS

On this frigid Christmas Eve, with a thirty-mile-per-hour wind blasting off Lake Erie, only 29,751 hardy souls are here in Cleveland's cavernous Municipal Stadium; more than 50,000 seats are vacant. What a pity—for never before has an NFL title game presented so intriguing a matchup.

The hometown Browns, named after their head coach Paul Brown, are the new boys on the block, and all season they have had to prove that they belong. When the rival All American Football Conference raised the white flag after the 1949 campaign, the NFL agreed to absorb three of its clubs: the Baltimore Colts, the San Francisco 49ers, and the Browns. Cleveland had been the powerhouse of the AAFC, winning the championship in each of the conference's four years while losing a total of four games. They did it with Marion Motley, a mammoth fullback who inspired comparison with the great Nagurski; with Bill Willis, a brilliant middle guard who showed that speed counted for more than weight at his position; and with Lou Groza, maturing into the finest field-goal kicker the game had ever seen. But most of all, they did it with the devastating passes of Otto Graham to ends Mac Speedie and Dante Lavelli.

But had the Browns merely been big fish in a small pond? Nearly everyone in the NFL thought so. George Preston Marshall, owner of the Washington Redskins, said, "The worst team in our league could beat the best in theirs." Yet on the first Sunday of the 1950 season, the Browns humiliated the NFL champion Eagles 35–10. Afterwards the Eagles' coach, Greasy Neale, referred to the Browns as a "basketball team"; so the next time the two teams met, Coach Brown ordered Graham not to throw a single pass. He didn't, and the Browns won again.

In fact, Cleveland's only two losses during the regular season came at the hands of the New York Giants, and produced a tie for the conference crown and a playoff game which the Browns won 8–3. The Los Angeles Rams also had to play an extra game to get here today. During the regular season they had lost twice to the Chicago Bears, then defeated them 24–14 in a playoff to repeat as conference champs.

If the Browns, who threw the ball one play out of three, are a basketball team, what are we to call the Rams? They passed more often than they ran, averaging thirty-eight tosses per game, while establishing new records for passing yardage, total yardage, and points. They defeated their opposition by such scores as 70–27, 65–24, 51–14, and 45–14. And in a game against Detroit they scored 41 points—*in the third quarter.* At the heart of the Rams' offense are quarterbacks Bob Waterfield and Norm Van Brocklin and receivers Tom Fears and Elroy Hirsch.

Ironically, the Rams too had their origin in an "outlaw" circuit, the American Football League of 1936, when their home town was . . . Cleveland. The Cleveland Rams were admitted into the NFL the following season, and only five years ago, behind the heroics of rookie quarterback Waterfield, won the championship right here on this field! In 1946 the Rams packed their bags and went west, leaving little love behind.

So who is to turn up his nose at whom? That's the question as Lou Groza tees up the ball (the Browns won the toss and chose the wind advantage). And we're off! The ball descends end over end to V. T. "Vitamin" Smith, a bowlegged little scatback who has returned three kickoffs for touchdowns. Not this time, though; Vitamin is swallowed up at the 18.

The gaudily outfitted Rams (gold jerseys and ram-horned helmets) open in a conventional full-house T, with all three backs—former Army All-American Glenn Davis, powerful fullback Dick Hoerner, and Smith—behind Waterfield. This initial test of the Browns' 5-3-3 defense was planned two weeks ago. L.A.'s offensive coach, Hamp Pool, had been viewing the Browns' game films when he noticed that Cleveland's right linebacker would key on the offense's left halfback—that is, if the back went out for a pass, the linebacker would cover him; but if the back stayed in to block, then the linebacker would double up on the left end. It is this tendency that Pool will seek to exploit.

As Waterfield barks the signals, Smith goes in motion to the right. At the snap from center Fred Naumetz, Waterfield fades to pass. Hoerner and Davis stay in to block. Right end Hirsch cuts outside. Left end Fears breaks over the middle—trailed by right linebacker Tony Adamle, as planned (see diagram). Davis holds his blocking position for only a moment, then flares a few steps and sprints upfield. Tommy James, the Browns' right cornerback who had moved toward the middle with Fears, reacts hurriedly and slips on the frozen turf. The fleet Davis glides by, catches the soft pass in the clear at his 45, and leads safety Ken Gorgal a merry chase all the way into the end zone.

An eighty-two-yard touchdown pass on the first play from scrimmage—this is unthinkable in a championship game, when

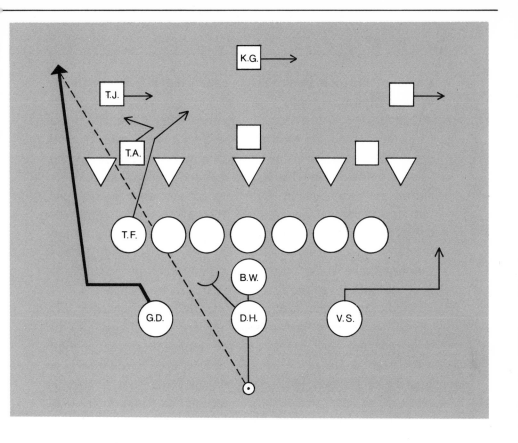

The Rams, operating from an uncharacteristic full-house T formation, take advantage of the Browns' pursuit on the very first play from scrimmage. The key maneuver is the inside cut of left end Tom Fears (T.F.), which lures the gambling right linebacker, Tony Adamle (T.A.), toward the middle. While Fears runs his route convincingly, Bob Waterfield (B.W.) fades to pass; Dick Hoerner (D.H.) steps up to block; and Vitamin Smith (V.S.), who had gone in motion before the snap, turns upfield. Glenn Davis (G.D.) is the intended beneficiary of all this movement; he delays, then flies up the sideline free as a bird. Defensive back Tommy James (T.J.) realizes that Fears has pulled him out of position, whirls, and slips. Safety Ken Gorgal (K.G.) had drifted a few steps to his left as Smith went in motion, and now cannot retrace the lost ground in time. Touchdown!

tradition and common sense dictate caution. How will the stunned Browns respond?

The answer is not long in coming. After Cleveland's Ken Carpenter returns the kickoff to the 30, Graham fights fire with fire. Three consecutive short completions—to right end Lavelli, to right halfback Dub Jones, and to Lavelli again—advance the ball to the Cleveland 46. Otto rolls left to pass a fourth time, but after a pump fake, he tucks the ball in and scampers for twenty-two yards. A plunge by Motley nets only a yard, but on second down Graham hits Jones on a flare-out and up, behind Tommy Keane, for a thirty-one-yard score. Groza provides the PAT and at 3:10 of the first quarter this racehorse game is 7–7.

Smith returns the kickoff only to the 19, where the L.A. offensive unit takes over. (This is the first year of free substitution, though a few players on each team will see action both ways today.) On first down Waterfield fires a square-out to Tom Fears for five. Fears has been the NFL's top receiver in each of the last three seasons, reaching his pinnacle in 1950 with a record eighty-four catches; an incredible eighteen of these came in a game against Green Bay. Shifty rather than fast, he runs his routes with such precision that no back can hope to cover him one-on-one. (The trouble is that Hirsch, on the opposite end, must also be double-covered because of his moves and speed; and with Davis set out as a flankerback, the Rams' passing attack can seem unstoppable.)

On second down Waterfield drops back yet again while Fears runs a corner route with a double fake—to the outside, then to the middle, and back toward the left corner. The ball is perfectly thrown. Fears runs under it for a forty-four-yard gain.

Now, with the ball on the 32, the Rams try the overland trail, and it works splendidly as well. The big gainer is a fifteen-yard burst to the 3 by Smith, through a hole created by left guard Jack Finlay. On the next play Dick Hoerner also follows Finlay to plunge over the goal line. Contrary to accepted practice, the Rams have used the pass to set up the run.

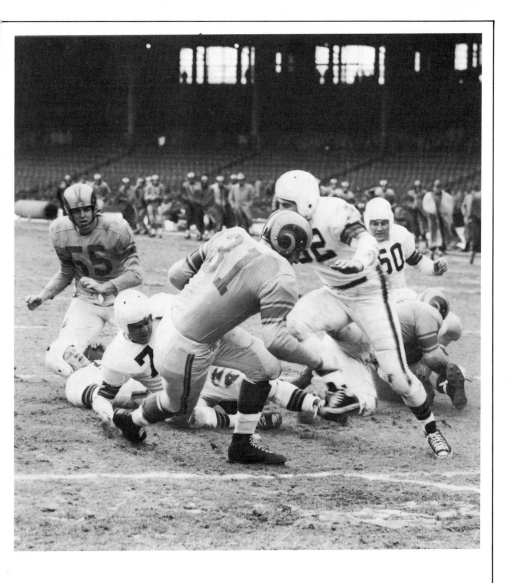

Los Angeles fullback Dick Hoerner falls over the goal line from the 3, capping an impressive first-period drive. In last year's title game, which the Eagles won 14-0, the Rams' attack had fizzled when heavy rains shut down the air lanes. To beat the Browns today, they must prove they can run with the ball as well as pass it.

Remarkably, neither team scores on its next possession. After an exchange of punts, the Browns take over on their 35. A pass to left end Mac Speedie is incomplete, but Woodley Lewis had his arms wrapped around Speedie before the ball arrived. The interference call puts the ball at midfield as the first period comes to a close. After Motley gains over the middle, Speedie collects a screen pass and hobbles to the L.A. 26. A great receiver who led the AAFC three straight years, Speedie cannot live up to his name today: He pulled a leg muscle in Thursday's practice, and his principal value to the Browns is as a decoy.

Graham is sacked for a loss to the 35, but goes for the bundle on the very next play. He sends Lavelli down the middle, where he splits defenders Lewis and Keane and races for paydirt with a half step advantage. He extends his arms at the 8, cradles the ball, and continues into the end zone. Groza readies for the automatic extra point with Tommy James to hold. But Hal Herring's snap sails high in a gust of wind and James must lunge to haul it in. Realizing that a kick would be blocked, James races to the right and throws to Tony Adamle in the end zone. Adamle gets his mitts on it, but cannot hold on. The Browns have missed their first PAT all season long, and the Rams retain the edge by one point: 14–13.

Ordinarily we might expect to see Norm Van Brocklin enter the game now; the second-year quarterback split duties with Waterfield during the season. In the playoff against Chicago, however, Van Brocklin broke a rib on the third play of the game and is being held out this afternoon. If the Rams are operating at less than peak efficiency, though, you'd have a hard time convincing Cleveland. With Waterfield firing passes to Fears and Hirsch, and sending Dick Hoerner through and around the confused Browns' line on delays, traps, and a Statue of Liberty, the Rams quickly bring the ball to the enemy 7.

The Browns cannot seem to stop the Rams, but fortunately for them the Rams blunder and stop themselves. After a holding penalty pushes them back to the 26, Waterfield sends Fears over the middle and underthrows him; Gorgal steps in front of Fears, scoops up the low throw at the 16, and returns thirty-three yards.

The Browns need to control the ball now, to pick up a few first downs and give their defense a breather. But three plays produce a loss of twelve, and Horace Gillom comes on to punt.

Hurrying to avoid a block, Gillom flubs the kick a mere nine yards; here come the Rams again. Waterfield throws to Fears for ten, then to Hirsch for eight. He fades again, holds the ball aloft as if to pass, and lets it be plucked from his hand by Smith, circling behind him in the Statue of Liberty. Cleveland's right end Len Ford smells the play coming, however, and nails Vitamin for a fourteen-yard loss. Big Len had just entered the game; he had not even taken part in a practice session since October 15, when a Chicago Cardinal slugged him in the jaw and broke it.

Ford's play is only a momentary setback. A personal foul against Cleveland and another pass to Fears soon have L.A. knocking at the door again. On third down and eight at the 10, Waterfield fakes a reverse and takes it up the middle himself, but is stopped at the 8. The Rams will have to settle for the easy field goal. But Waterfield, usually a reliable placekicker, sees his attempt from the 16 drift wide. The Browns have slipped off the hook once more. Badly outplayed in this quarter, they are delighted to trail by only one point at intermission.

Coaches Paul Brown and Joe Stydahar review the events of the first half with their assistants, and offer words of wisdom to their players. But most of all, I suspect, the teams welcome halftime for the chance to get out of the biting cold.

Whatever coach Brown tells his Brownies at the half, it works. The Browns receive the kickoff and zip through the Rams' defense. The key play is a twenty-nine-yard screen pass to Gillom, who has replaced the ailing Speedie for the second half. Then, with the ball on the Los Angeles 39, Graham flares both halfbacks, thus tying up the L.A. backs; Gillom hooks over the middle, taking a safety with him and leaving poor

Tommy Keane to cover Lavelli by himself, an impossible task. Otto lifts a lob pass to Lavelli, running a post pattern. Keane's desperate leap for the ball is short by inches, and the Browns regain the lead, 20–14. The question now is whether coach Brown has similarly inspired his defense.

Smith returns Groza's kick to the 29, and Waterfield peppers the Cleveland secondary anew. He fires passes to Smith and Fears for a first down at his 45, then tosses to Smith for thirty-eight yards. Denied twice inside the 10-yard line in the second quarter, the Rams now replace guile with force. The ball goes to Hoerner for eight, then one, and then three; first down at the 5. Three more carries by the six-foot-four-inch fullback take the ball to the 1. The team trails by six, and Waterfield did miss that chippie in the second quarter, so Stydahar has his team go for it. The call is to Hoerner for the seventh straight time, and he crashes over for the touchdown. Waterfield adds the point: 21–20.

Woodley Lewis's kickoff is downed in the end zone for a touchback. From the 20 Graham pitches to Motley, who has been held in check by the surprisingly staunch L.A. line (the Rams allowed their opponents a whopping 25 points per game this year). The NFL's leading rusher in 1950, this 238-pound tank will finish the day with a mere six carries for nine yards. Motley is the only Brown back to wear cleats on the frozen turf —the others wear sneakers. He circles left end and gets out past the 25 before he is hemmed in by tacklers. Perhaps frustrated by his inactivity in the first half, he reverses field, giving up ground to the 14 as he awaits blockers. But before his linemen can regroup to aid him, Motley is caught in a pincers action by Ram ends Larry Brink and Jack Zilly. The ball squirts loose, bouncing back to the 6 where Brink picks it up and trots into the end zone. In twenty-one seconds, the Browns have transformed a 20–14 lead into a 28–20 deficit. The icy stadium is silent.

Seemingly demoralized, the Browns come up empty on the next three downs and punt. The Rams smell blood and stay aggressive, threatening again.

But again the gods smile on the Browns at the moment of their impending doom. Just a minute before the end of the quarter, Warren Lahr leaps to pick off a Waterfield pass at the 21 and brings it back to the 35. There is still plenty of time, but the ground game has not worked at all. Coach Brown, who sends in all the plays for Graham through alternating messenger guards, decides to move upfield through the air, but not by throwing deep and hoping to get rich quick—an interception now could be fatal. Brown prefers the safe pass to the sideline: the receiver goes downfield five or ten yards, then cuts outside; but instead of turning at a right angle, he comes back toward the line of scrimmage, gaining a step or two on the defensive back that cannot be made up.

It is precisely this sort of pass that Graham throws to Lavelli for five straight completions covering only twenty-two yards. At the L.A. 43, with fourth down and one yard to go, Graham sneaks for three. Then a combination of five rushes and three more passes to Lavelli puts the ball on the 14. One of the passes is a seven-yarder completed on fourth and four; one of the runs is a three-yard rollout by Graham on fourth and three.

On almost every play this quarter the Browns have been lining up in a double-flanker, with Rex Bumgardner set wide to the left, Jones to the right, and only Motley behind the quarterback as a potential blocker. This formation puts tremendous pressure on the Rams' 5-2-4 defense, particularly the linebackers, who are forced to cover one or both of the backs one-on-one. With the ball at the 14, Graham spots Bumgardner cutting for the left corner of the end zone, blanketed by linebacker Fred Naumetz. He throws the ball low. Bumgardner reaches out to make a nifty catch, keeping his feet in bounds for the critical moment, then careening into a snowbank on the sideline. Groza adds the point, and the Browns close the gap to 28–27, with ten and a half minutes to play.

Two uneventful possessions follow, each culminated by a booming punt; Gillom cans one for sixty-eight yards, making

Otto Graham (60) tries to shake-and-bake Woodley Lewis. The interesting part of the play, however, is occurring behind them, where Dante Lavelli is offering a knuckle sandwich to Dick Huffman.

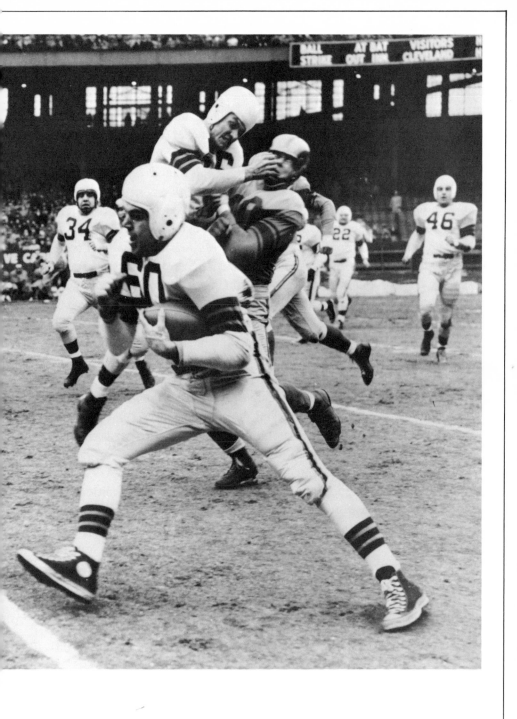

up for the nine-yarder earlier, and Waterfield contributes to his fifty-yard average for the day, a championship record. On the Rams' next crack at the ball Waterfield, not sitting on his slim lead, puts the ball in the air—but linebacker Tommy Thompson dives to intercept at the L.A. 47. Is this the break that will turn the game around for the final time? Cleveland fans squirm in their seats.

Graham throws a twenty-two-yarder to Jones; the Browns are well within range for a go-ahead field goal. Now Graham bootlegs the ball around left end—but is blasted from the blind side and coughs up the ball! Mike Lazetich recovers for the Rams at the 24, and a disconsolate Graham trudges off the field with only three minutes to play.

As he reaches the bench with his head down, Graham is met by coach Brown, who pats him on the back. "Don't worry about it," Brown says. "We're going to get them anyway." Brown is not a dreamer—he knows that the Rams will now try to play the clock, and that if the defense can hold them, the offense should get one last crack. And more important, he knows what kind of a quarterback he has in Graham. Otto had entered Northwestern University on a basketball scholarship—oddly appropriate, considering his later success in the AAFC, the "basketball league"—before going on to Big Ten stardom in football. Brown was coaching Ohio State when he first noticed Otto; as soon as Brown was offered the helm of the Cleveland entry in the yet-to-be-founded AAFC, he knew that Graham was the man he wanted to run his T offense, even though Graham had been a single-wing tailback in college. Otto learned the mechanics of the T so well that in his ten years as a pro he led the Browns to the championship game *all ten times.*

As expected, the Rams keep the ball on the ground, hoping to pick up at least one first down while using up precious seconds. But Hoerner hits the Cleveland line twice for no gain, and on third and ten Davis's slant off right tackle yields only six yards. Waterfield booms a fifty-four-yard howitzer to the Browns'

16; Cliff Lewis fields it and dashes up to the 32, where he steps out of bounds. The clock shows 1:48 to play.

Graham fades to pass but finds no one open. With only Motley back to block, he cannot linger in the pocket waiting for a receiver to break free—a sack would be devastating now. Tucking the ball under his arm, Otto shows his single-wing training, bolting outside around the rushing right end for 14 yards, stepping out of bounds on the Cleveland 46.

Fading again, he spots Bumgardner open in the left flat and hits him for fifteen; Rex skips out on the L.A. 39. Now Otto drops back a bit deeper to give himself a little more time—he's going for the big one, to Jones in the end zone. But Dub is well covered by Naumetz, who actually has a better shot at the ball. The pass hangs; it looks as if it's to be intercepted, assuring a Ram win . . . but Naumetz's frigid fingers can't hold it, and the ball drops to earth.

Thus reprieved, Graham fires to Jones for seventeen, placing the ball on the L.A. 22, once again well inside Lou Groza's range. With a minute left, will Coach Brown call for running plays to wind down the clock and position the ball between the goalposts?

No. Graham again finds Bumgardner open in the left flat after beating his defender on a Z-out pattern. Rex steps out at the 11 and stumbles into the snowbank with only forty seconds remaining. Brown now calls for a handoff to Bumgardner solely to move the ball in from the left hashmark and afford a better kicking angle. In the huddle, however, Bumgardner suggests that Otto keep the ball himself. Rex's hands are wet and cold from falling in the snow. "I was afraid I might fumble," he will say after the game. "I knew Otto wouldn't."

And Otto doesn't, moving the ball toward the center and forward one yard. With Hal Herring poised to snap, Tommy James kneeling to hold at the 16, and Lou Groza standing two and a half steps behind the placement, the game hangs in the balance. The snap is true, the hold flawless, and the kick . . .

All eyes are on the ball as it makes its way from Lou Groza's toe toward the crossbar. Even the umpire, who should be on the lookout for infractions in the line, can't resist a peek.

perfect! Thousands of fans stream down from their seats and onto the field. The police try to shoo them to the sidelines, for though the Browns are in front 30–28, twenty seconds remain to be played.

Order is restored, and the teams line up for the kickoff. Groza's boot is taken at the 12 by Jerry Williams who, incredibly, nearly breaks away before being tackled at his 47. As the Rams' offense races onto the field, we notice that something has changed. Number 7, Waterfield, is not coming out. Standing over center is Number 25, Norm Van Brocklin, cracked rib and all. He will throw one long bomb and concern himself with the pain during the off-season.

Norman fades back to his 40 and fires the ball some fifty-five yards in the direction of Glenn Davis, who is covered tightly by Warren Lahr. At the 5, Lahr and Davis leap for the bomb. Lahr comes away with it for his second intercept of the afternoon, but Davis continues to grapple for the ball while dragging Lahr into the end zone. Will he wrest the pass away for a touchdown? Will the officials rule a safety? Neither—the play is whistled dead at the 5 as the clock runs out.

The team from the other side of the tracks has done it. They have defended the honor of all those who struggled for recognition in the old AAFC, and established themselves as the class of the NFL for years to come. The Rams? They can hold their heads high after an effort like this, and their revenge will be sweet in next year's championship match. But this day belongs to the outcasts, the upstarts, the revolutionaries—the Browns.

SCORING

RAMS	14	0	14	0 — 28
BROWNS	7	6	7	10 — 30

L.A.: Davis, 82, pass from Waterfield (Waterfield, kick).
Cle.: Jones, 31, pass from Graham (Groza, kick).
L.A.: Hoerner, 3, run (Waterfield, kick).
Cle.: Lavelli, 35, pass from Graham (bad snap).
Cle.: Lavelli, 39, pass from Graham (Groza, kick).
L.A.: Hoerner, 1, run (Waterfield, kick).
L.A.: Brink, 6, fumble return (Waterfield, kick).
Cle.: Bumgardner, 14, pass from Graham (Groza, kick).
Cle.: Groza, FG, 16.

TEAM STATISTICS

	Rams	Browns
First downs	22	22
Rushing yardage	106	116
Passing yardage	301	257
Punt return yardage	14	22
Passes	18-32	22-33
Interceptions by	1	5
Punts	4-51	5-38
Fumbles lost	0	3
Yards penalized	48	25

INDIVIDUAL STATISTICS

RUSHES—L.A.: Hoerner, 24 for 86 yards; Davis, 6 for 6; Smith, 4 for 11; Pasquari-
ello, 1 for 1; Waterfield, 1 for 2. Cle.: Graham, 12 for 99; Motley, 6 for 9;
Bumgardner, 5 for 2; Jones, 2 for 4; Lavelli, 0 for 2 (lateral from Graham).
PASSES—L.A.: Waterfield, 18 of 31 for 312 yards; Van Brocklin, 0 of 1. Cle.: Graham,
22 of 33 for 298.
RECEPTIONS—L.A.: Fears, 9 for 136 yards; Hirsch, 4 for 42; Smith, 3 for 46; Davis,
2 for 88. Cle.: Lavelli, 11 for 128; Jones, 4 for 80; Bumgardner, 4 for 46;
Gillom, 1 for 29; Speedie, 1 for 17; Motley, 1 for —2.

December 28, 1958

BALTIMORE COLTS

VS.

NEW YORK GIANTS

Just as the 1950 championship game could be described as a battle between two Cleveland clubs—the one that went west and the one that stayed behind—so can today's title match be viewed as a contest of two teams from New York. How this oddity came to be is a twisty tale, pointing up the final growing pains of a sport entering upon its golden age.

The Colts, you'll recall, were one of three AAFC franchises absorbed by the NFL in 1950. But while the Browns went on to claim the crown, the Colts stumbled into oblivion. They won only one game and at season's end disbanded, their better players scattered among the remaining twelve teams: for example, quarterback Y. A. Tittle went to San Francisco, lineman Art Spinney went to Cleveland, and halfback Buddy Young went to the New York Yankees. In 1951 the Yankees replaced the Colts as the artistic and financial flop of the league; they were sold to a group from Dallas and became the Texans. But in 1952, after four home games played in relative privacy, the new owners dumped the Texans in the league's lap and the team played out its schedule on the road. So in 1953 Baltimore, hungering for a pro team after two years without, took in the homeless "Yankee-Texan" waifs and renamed them the Colts.

A ragtag bunch of raw recruits, long-shot castoffs, and shell-shocked survivors from Dallas and New York, the Colts brought up the bottom of the NFL for a few years while Coach Weeb Ewbank tried to mold them into contenders. When he was hired off the Cleveland staff in 1954, he promised a championship-caliber club in five years. Now he has delivered. The team he brings into Yankee Stadium today is a powerhouse, boasting the league's top offense and a defense second only to that of their opponents this balmy Sunday, the New York Giants. Yet national media recognition has eluded them—Baltimore's best players labor in the shadows while even New York's journeymen bask in the limelight.

In the locker room moments ago, Ewbank played to this sore spot, reminding his men of how far they had come to reach this day: of the indignities that Art Donovan had suffered on this very field as a Yankee in 1951; of the humiliation Gino Marchetti had endured as a Dallas Texan forced to play a "home" game in Akron, Ohio; of the double dose of insult heaped on Art Spinney—going down with the original NFL Colts in 1950, being chosen by Cleveland in the dispersal draft, then being bounced back to Baltimore in 1953 without ever having played for the Browns. All three have subsequently become all-pro linemen, but these wounds were still fresh enough for Ewbank to rub salt in them. He went through the whole team: linebacker Bill Pellington, cut by the Browns; defensive back Carl Taseff, a throw-in in a massive housecleaning trade; even all-pro quarterback Johnny Unitas, rejected by Notre Dame before enrolling at Louisville, then cut by the Steelers and relegated to the Bloomfield Rams of the sandlots, where the Colts spotted him. Though the Colts clinched their division with two weeks yet to play and are favored to win today, every one of them, Ewbank said, has something to prove.

Stung by that pregame address, the Colts line up at their 40 to set play in motion before a packed house and a national television audience. Bert Rechichar (another Cleveland discard) booms the ball five yards deep into the end zone, where Giant rookie Don Maynard downs it for a touchback.

At the helm of New York's much-maligned offense right now is young Don Heinrich. A 38-percent-passer, he customarily starts the game while veteran Charlie Conerly sizes up the situation from the sidelines, awaiting the lightning bolt of wisdom that will enable him to take the field and lead his men to victory. Neither Heinrich nor Conerly much likes this system of coach Jim Lee Howell's, but there's no arguing with success—two years ago it did bring the Giants a championship.

Hoping to surprise the Colts, Heinrich takes to the air. On first down his pass to left end Kyle Rote is batted down by Marchetti. His second-down pass, to halfback Alex Webster in the right flat, is good for seven yards. And on third and three, with Baltimore bunched at the line for the run, Heinrich throws again, to Rote crossing over the middle; but Taseff breaks it up.

Taking over on their 30 after a forty-three-yard punt by Don Chandler, the Colts open in more conservative fashion. Lenny Moore, the most dangerous halfback in football, sweeps left but is dropped for a three-yard loss by cornerback Carl Karilivacz. Fullback Alan "the Horse" Ameche gains seven through the middle, bringing up a third down and six. Unitas, the league's top passer this year, drops back while surveying the defense. The receivers are all covered—he must make the first down on his own. Three yards past the scrimmage line, however, he is mugged by middle linebacker Sam Huff, the man who personifies defense in this town; the ball pops loose and is pounced upon by safety

Jim Patton. As it has done so many times this season, the Giant defense has given the offense a short field to work with. In fact, it is the 4–3 defense, installed by assistant coach Tom Landry, that has brought the Giants to this championship game. As in 1950, the Giants defeated Cleveland twice to produce a tie for the conference crown; but this time around they won the playoff, too, shutting out the Browns while holding the great Jim Brown to eight yards in seven carries.

Webster tries off tackle but is stopped for a loss of one. Now Heinrich takes the snap and turns—without the football! The ball is batted around by scrambling linemen to the Colt 45, where Marchetti falls on it. Opportunity has knocked on New York's door and gone begging.

Unitas swings a four-yard pass out to right halfback L. G. (Louis George, alias "Long Gone") Dupre, then hands to Dupre for a one-yard gain to midfield. On third and five, Johnny U. throws to tight end Jim Mutscheller at the sideline—but Karilivacz cuts in front to intercept, returning to the N.Y. 45.

Does anybody want the ball? Does anybody want to score? For a great game, this one sure is off to a wretched start.

At last Frank Gifford, the Giants' leading rusher and receiver, gets his hands on the ball, but New York still cannot move. Chandler punts back to Baltimore.

With the ball on his own 15, Unitas fades, pumps once, then heaves deep to Lenny Moore, who thus far has been covered one-on-one by left cornerback Lindon Crow. Crow races along step-for-step, but the ball is perfectly thrown: Moore makes the catch at the Giant 40, and shakes free for fifteen more before being tackled by Patton. Though the play gains sixty yards, it is more important for the change it prompts in New York's defensive alignment—Moore will not receive single coverage again this afternoon, which means that left end Raymond Berry's side of the field will be rendered more vulnerable.

Stopped at the 25, the Colts call on Steve Myhra, their erratic placekicker, to attempt a 32-yard field goal. His kick is wide but

The best quarterback who ever played the game? Votes might go to Sammy Baugh, or Otto Graham, or Fran Tarkenton, or Roger Staubach. But chances are that this man, John Unitas, would collect the most ballots of all. He had style, *too.*

the Giants, continuing to make mistakes by the bushelful, are offside; Myhra will try again from the 27.

At the snap, left guard Art Spinney turns outside for a block on the charging Sam Huff—but Huff is coming up the middle, and knifes through the gap to block the kick. Jim Katcavage recovers for New York at the 22.

Oh, this is awful. Wait . . . a roar is rising from the stands as the Giant offensive platoon straggles onto the field . . . Number 42, Charlie Conerly, has come on to try his hand. Nearly booed back to Mississippi as a young quarterback, Charlie has become ever more popular with each new gray hair. He too comes out throwing: first a misfired slant-in to Webster, then a lob to fullback Mel Triplett for nine. On third and one, he sends Gifford around left end behind Roosevelt Brown, the perennial all-pro tackle. A great block by Rote wipes out the linebacker, and Gifford is off to the races. Only a desperate lunge by Milt Davis slows Gifford's progress, enabling the Colts to corral Frank after a thirty-eight-yard run to the Baltimore 31.

Triplett hits the left side for two. Conerly fires to Rote, incomplete. Given ample time by the Giant line, he fades back again. Webster has floated downfield behind the Colt secondary. The pass is in the air, on target, and . . . Webster . . . slips. The ball flutters by, a sure touchdown lost. Onto the field comes kicker Pat Summerall, the hero of the regular season's final game, when he boomed a field goal forty-nine yards through a driving snowstorm to defeat the Browns in the final minute of play. This attempt will come from the 36, under less melodramatic conditions. And it is good, giving the Giants a 3–0 lead.

The Colts fail to move on their next possession, punting to the N.Y. 18 on the final play of this remarkably untidy first quarter. Opening the second period, Conerly finds his favorite receiver, Gifford, at the left sideline behind a wall of blockers. Perhaps a little impatient to get underway, Gifford catches the ball but does not tuck it in securely—as cornerback Johnny

Sample hits him, the pigskin pops out and is recovered at the 20 by Gene "Big Daddy" Lipscomb.

Now Unitas attacks the middle of the Giant defense with three straight running plays, producing a first down at the 10. Then Moore takes the handoff and turns left end—he seems to have clear sailing ahead, but is stopped at the 2 by Patton's grab around the ankles.

When the Colts get this close to paydirt there's little doubt where the play is coming—over Jim Parker, one of the all-time greats at tackle and, later in his career, guard. Big Jim knocks Rosey Grier back into the end zone; Ameche waltzes in for the score, and Myhra adds the point: Colts 7, Giants 3.

A completion to Rote on the next series moves the Giants to their own 48, but they are driven back. Chandler's punt sails into the arms of Jackie Simpson at the 10—and through them, to be retrieved by the Giants' Mel Guy. Let's see—that makes an interception, a blocked kick, and three fumbles, in a game only twenty minutes old.

Make that four fumbles. On New York's first play from the 10, Gifford is separated from the ball by defensive end Don Joyce, who falls on the prize at the 14 as Yankee Stadium emits a king-sized groan.

With his back to his own goal line, Unitas loads up on first down and heaves the ball some 50 yards downfield for Dupre, incomplete. Having thus captured the Giants' attention, he now sets his sights more modestly, linking up with Berry for five yards. Berry, an unimposing physical specimen who wears contact lenses and a back brace and whose legs are not the same length, is nevertheless the league's top pass-catcher this year. Diligent—some would say maniacal—practice, study, and discipline have made him a worthy successor to Tom Fears as the most accomplished end of his day.

A toss to Ameche produces a first down at the 29. Moore zips around right end for ten more and another first. Ameche for six, Moore for three, Ameche for two. This is shaping up as the

With the Colts' fearsome end, Gino Marchetti, about to flatten him, Charlie Conerly wisely unloads the ball in the general direction of end Kyle Rote. The pass will fall incomplete, but Charlie will live to try again.

first sustained drive of the game. On third and seven from the New York 46, Johnny U. is chased out of the pocket but manages to scramble for sixteen yards. The fans are still hoping that the defense can come up big.

But the Giants are on the run now, scurrying to plug each leak just as another one springs. A pass to Berry clicks to the 21. On third down Ameche, needing one, splits the line for six. Unitas again sends his fullback into the line, drawing the linebackers and cornerbacks in a step. But the Horse does not have the ball. Spinning after the fake, Unitas shuffles back a few steps and finds Berry in the end zone, free as can be. Touchdown!

Eighty-six yards in fourteen plays: It is an impressive performance, inspiring to the 15,000 or so Baltimore faithful here today, dispiriting to the nearly 50,000 others, especially the Giants. They decline to run the kickoff out of the end zone, then kill the final minute of the half. Trailing 14–3, they head to the locker room knowing the task that lies ahead, yet doubting their ability to perform it.

At the half, the Giants revise their strategy. Offensive assistant Vince Lombardi suggests using Gifford primarily as a decoy for the second half. Since the Colts have assigned two men to dog his steps on all plays, sending him away from the ball should leave the Colts shorthanded at the point of action. The defensive strategy? No change—just keep hitting and hope for mistakes.

The Colts receive the kickoff but fail to move. Let's see if New York's offense, which produced only two first downs in the opening thirty minutes, wakes up. Conerly hands to Gifford —no gain. He passes to Gifford in the flat—a loss of three. He fades to pass again and is buried by the Colt line—a loss of five. The new strategy looks the same as the old strategy, with the same results. Chandler punts, and Moore's fair catch gives Baltimore the ball on its own 41.

Going right for the jugular, Unitas whips a pass to Mutscheller for thirty-two yards. A sideline to Berry and a slant-in by Moore, who drives Crow back in fear of the bomb, provide a first down at the 3. The Giants mass on the line to stop the run; Ameche drives for two. Only a yard stands between Baltimore and a rout. Unitas tries to sneak across behind Parker, but Modzelewski, Grier, and Huff stop him for no gain. Ameche bangs off right guard, but Huff and Mo hold the fort again.

Fourth and still one. The kicking team will not be sent in. In the huddle Unitas calls "Flow 28," a play on which Moore will be set out in the left slot and Ameche will line up as a halfback. Unitas will pitch to the Horse, who will either run wide right into the end zone or, if the defense closes on him, flip a pass to Mutscheller. The only drawback to this play is that Ameche has never thrown a pass in professional football—so when left line-backer Cliff Livingston reads "run" and charges at him, leaving Mutscheller wide open, Ameche fails to pull the trigger and is lassoed at the 5.

The magnificent goal-line stand has the place rocking with new hope. The Giants have averted a blowout, for the moment.

On first down Gifford gains five. Webster bulls up the middle for three, to the 13. New York must get the first down—to give its defense a breather, to obtain a better field position if eventually they must punt, but most of all to keep the momentum of this game from swinging immediately and forcefully back to the Colts. Two yards to go; Conerly fakes a pitch to Gifford, retreats, and flips a pass over the middle to Rote at the N.Y. 40. As the fans jump to their feet, Rote shakes one, two tacklers and gallops on. Andy Nelson finally grabs him at the 30 and rides him down at the 25—where Rote fumbles! The ball bounces, however, right into the hands of Alex Webster, trailing the play, who lugs it all the way down to the 1. Anticlimactically, Triplett bulls over on first down and Summerall adds the point. A daring call and a timely bit of luck have left the Giants trailing by only 14–10.

As the Colts take the field after the kickoff, the defense can't wait to get at them. Modzelewski sacks Unitas once and pres-

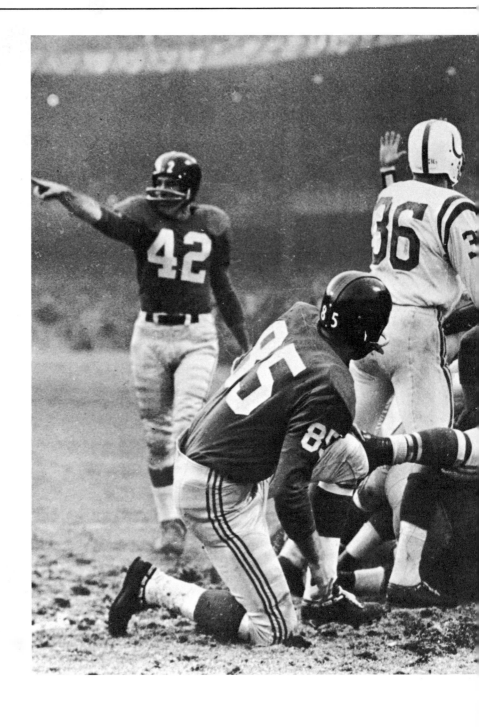

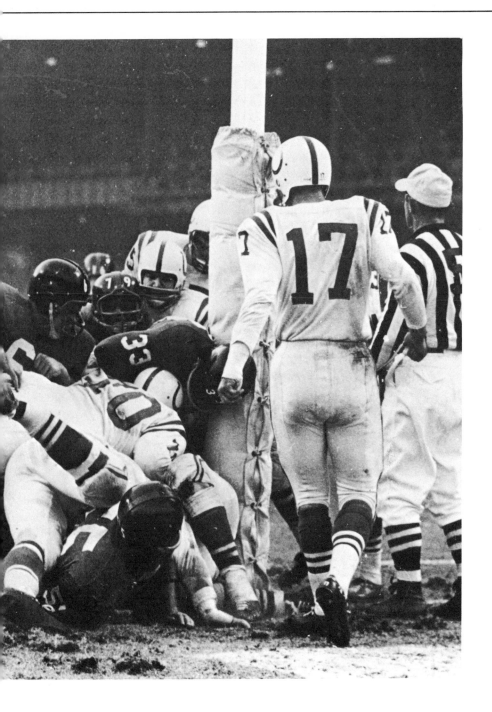

Does Mel Triplett (33) get over? Conerly looks to the right side of the field, where another official stands with arms upraised—the Giants are back in the game!

sures him out of the pocket another time. Baltimore must punt.

From the N.Y. 19, Webster probes the middle for three. Next, Conerly fakes a pitch to him, holding the linebackers, and pops a seventeen-yard pass over the middle to tight end Bob Schnelker. Growing more intrepid in his play selection, Conerly calls for a pass off a double fake reverse, with both backs crossing but neither receiving the handoff. Again he finds Schnelker over the middle, this time for a fat forty-six-yard gain. Before the Colts' secondary can collect their wits, the Giants line up strong to the right, isolating left half Gifford on a linebacker. Giff catches the pass at the 5 and drags tackler Milt Davis into the end zone. Less than one minute into the fourth period, the Giants take the lead, 17–14.

The tide has turned; Unitas must try to reverse it again. Coolly, he hits Moore and then Berry. A pass interference ruling against Crow advances the ball to New York's 38. Here the Giants stiffen, however, and Bert Rechichar comes on for a forty-six-yard field-goal attempt. Myhra handles the chip shots, Rechichar the long ones—he once kicked a fifty-six-yarder, the NFL record at this point. But today his kick falls short; New York takes over at the 20.

After moving past midfield in brisk fashion the Giants revert to their first-half form: rookie halfback Phil King, in for Webster, fumbles at the Colt 42. Several players chase the bounding ball, inadvertently kicking it back toward the Giant goal. Colts' reserve end Ordell Braase eventually covers the fumble at New York's 42.

Unitas tries to capitalize on the Giants' disarray by immediately going for six. He sends Moore straight upfield to challenge Crow yet again, and completes the bomb at the goal line . . . but out of bounds, according to the officials. Moore protests in vain. A sideline pattern to Berry is broken up by Karilivacz, then Unitas comes right back to Raymond for a first down at the 31. Dupre darts to the 27. But now Andy Robustelli, the Giants' all-pro end, breaks past Parker for the first time to throw Unitas for an eleven-yard loss. Modzelewski follows with another sack at the N.Y. 47, forcing a punt. The defense has bailed out the offense again.

Taking over at their 19, the Giants will try to stay on the ground and deny Baltimore another crack at the ball. Webster lumbers off tackle for five, but Gifford follows for no gain. Bravely, Conerly goes to the air; Webster circles out of the backfield and catches the pass for ten. At this moment up in the pressbox, with just over three minutes left, Charlie Conerly is being voted the MVP of this championship game, an honor which carries with it a new 1959 Chevy Corvette.

But with 2:30 left, it may be premature to slam the coffin lid on the Colts. On third down and four at the 40, Conerly gives to Gifford on a power sweep right, with both guards pulling and Webster leading Frank to the hole (this is a play which will make a hero of Paul Hornung in the next decade). Webster crunches Taseff, coming up from the cornerback spot, and Gifford cuts inside. But Schnelker cannot hold out Marchetti, who tramples him to grab Giff. While these two tussle, middle linebacker Don Shinnick crosses over to straighten Gifford up, then the six-foot-six-inch, 290-pound Lipscomb, pursuing from the other side of the line, crushes the entire tableau.

The bottom line: Marchetti's right leg is snapped above the ankle, and Gifford is short of the first down by six inches (though more than twenty years later, he's still not convinced). Some of the Giants gesture to coach Howell that they want to go for the first down, but Howell sees that as a foolish gamble, especially when he has a punter like Chandler. What do you think? Don seems to bear out his coach's wisdom, as he boots a beauty, forty-six yards with no return.

There is 1:56 on the clock, and the Colts must start on their 14 with only one timeout left. The Giants line up in the 1950s version of the "prevent" defense, protecting the sidelines and the deep areas. On first down Unitas throws incomplete to Mutscheller. On second down Dupre runs a buttonhook pattern, turning back for the ball—but drops it. The crowd is yelling louder with each play, if that is possible. The Giants are one down short of forcing a punt—but here Unitas catches fire. He hits Moore for eleven crucial yards to sustain the Colts' chances. After another incompletion to Dupre, he connects with Berry on a hook-and-whirl to midfield; then Berry on a spectacular leaping catch to the 35; and Berry on a slant-and-spin to the 13. These four catches move the ball seventy-three yards; the Giants are still waiting for the sideline pass.

With twenty seconds left and the ball on the 13, the field-goal unit races on. Center Buzz Nutter sends a tight spiral to holder George Shaw, who spins the laces toward the goalposts. Myhra meets the ball cleanly and, at 0:07, drives it squarely between the uprights. Barring a miracle, we're about to have a tie, the first ever in an NFL championship.

Maynard returns the kickoff to the 18, and on the final play Conerly falls on the ball. Most of the players think the game is over, but we are going into a sudden-death overtime, in which the first team to score will win. The rulesmakers provided for this cruel manner of deciding deadlocked postseason contests eleven years ago but never—until now—has it been necessary.

After a three-minute intermission, the Giants win the coin toss and opt to receive; Rechichar's low line-drive kick brings Maynard up to the 10, where he tries for a shoestring catch and fails. Luckily, the ball bounces true, right into his arms, and he makes it up to the 20. On first down Gifford hits the left side for four. Now Conerly fakes to Triplett and throws for Schnelker. This is the Giants' opportunity—they must be aggressive. The pass is underthrown; Schnelker comes back for it, dives, but cannot gather it in. Third and six. Fading to pass again, Charlie is chased out of the pocket and hobbles around right end—an Otto Graham he is not. At the 29 he is hit by Pellington, then by Shinnick, and collapses two feet shy of the first down. Taseff fields Chandler's soaring drive at the 19, advancing it a yard.

Now Unitas will see if he can sustain the brilliance that produced this overtime period. Only twenty-five years old and only three years removed from the roster of the semipro Bloomfield Rams, he is being asked to stay cool in pro football's all-time pressure cooker. You'd think that the older, more experienced Conerly might have the advantage in this situation; but then again, no one has had any experience in a situation like this.

The Giant defenders bunch up at the line, daring Unitas to throw. Dupre sweeps the right side for eleven, and now Unitas will take up the dare. He sends Moore straight upfield on the fly pattern that has so worried Lindon Crow today. Though Moore has half a step on Crow, the Giant makes a valiant effort, extending himself at the last moment to tip the ball away. Next, Unitas sends Ameche in motion, knowing that Huff will follow him, and slips the handoff to Dupre on a draw through the vacated spot. The hole opens up, but closes quickly and Dupre gains only two. On third and eight, Unitas looks for Berry; seeing right linebacker Svare following Raymond in double coverage, he flips a pass in the left flat to Ameche, who barely makes the first down.

Dupre gains three to the 44. Backpedaling to pass, Johnny U. is unable to evade the onrushing Modzelewski and eats an eight-yard loss. Third and fifteen, time for a rabbit out of the hat: a formation not yet seen today, in which both ends are split wide and Moore, the primary receiver on this play, occupies the right slot. Moore is covered, so Unitas looks to the other side for Berry. Karilivacz, playing behind him, has slipped! Raymond does not know this but Unitas, rolling left away from the rush, motions Berry downfield past the first-down marker; oblivious to the blue jerseys descending upon him, he casually lays the ball in to Berry for twenty-one yards. What a show he is putting on!

Now Modzelewski will pay for that last sack. Unitas calls a trap play. While right tackle George Preas fires out to get Huff, right guard Sandusky and center Nutter diverge, creating a hole to let Mo charge through. Then Spinney, the left guard, cuts

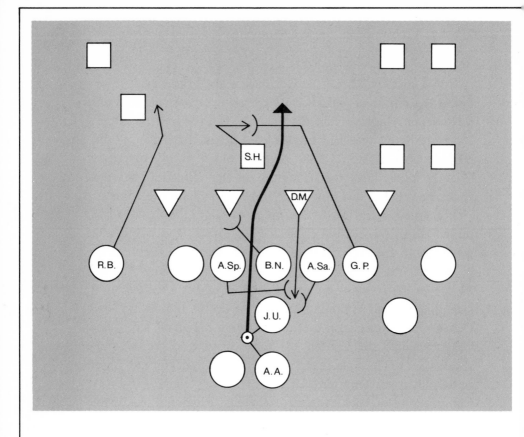

The trap play is an excellent call against a defensive lineman who has been beating his man with ego-inflating regularity. In this case Dick Modzelewski (D.M.), who has registered three sacks this afternoon, is the intended victim. Johnny Unitas (J.U.) turns to hand off to fullback Alan Ameche (A.A.); meanwhile the trap is being set. Center Buzz Nutter (B.N.) and right guard Alex Sandusky (A.Sa.) create a gap for Modzelewski to blow through. But left guard Art Spinney (A.Sp.) has pulled out of the line behind Nutter, and as soon as Mo sets foot in the backfield, Spinney and Sandusky lower the boom. Ameche breaks through the line and into the secondary. Middle linebacker Sam Huff (S.H.), who had drifted right to help cover Raymond Berry (R.B.), is taken out by George Preas (G.P.). The play goes for twenty-three yards.

behind Nutter to chop down Modzelewski (see diagram). Unitas hands to Ameche, who sees a path as wide as Fifth Avenue, and saunters twenty-three yards before the secondary can bring him down. The Colts are on New York's 20. Will they simply hit the middle and protect the ball, now that they are within field-goal range?

Unitas has not moved his team this far by doing what is expected. After a timeout to restore television transmission across the country (a cable broke), Dupre bounces off Katcavage for no gain; then Unitas hits Berry on a slant-in to the 8. This is Berry's twelfth catch of the game, surpassing the championship-game record set by Dante Lavelli in 1950.

Can the defense perform one more miracle? The fans bellow their encouragement as Ameche takes the handoff to the right, then cuts inside—only to be wrapped up by Huff after a gain of one. With the Giants blockading the line for the certain run, Unitas sends Mutscheller out to the right sideline and brazenly flips the ball to him, over the head of Cliff Livingston, for a gain to the 1.

Unitas will say after the game that had Livingston been step-for-step with Mutscheller, he would simply have thrown the ball over both of their heads and out of bounds. But what if a lineman had broken through to tip his arm? The ball might have wobbled into the arms of a Giant with ninety-plus yards of open country ahead.

It is third down, and one yard to go, and Baltimore will not be stopped now. Even on this most basic of plays, Unitas will go against the grain: rather than send Ameche via the customary route over left tackle Parker, he directs him to a hole on the right side. Mutscheller and Moore pick up the blitzing secondary men, and Sandusky and Preas open an enormous hole. At eight minutes and fifteen seconds of sudden-death overtime, the Colts win, 23–17.

They have won the game that, in the years to come, will be

The end of the thirteen-play, eighty-yard drive. Alan Ameche barrels into the end zone untouched, thanks to such fine blocks as the one Lenny Moore (24) throws on Emlen Tunnell. Safety Jim Patton (20) can do nothing but watch.

credited as the spark to America's obsession with pro football. Many will also call it the greatest football game ever played. We may think so, too, but let's hold off judgment; seven contenders for that title remain to be seen.

If the Colts actually had anything to prove today—Ewbank's oratory aside—then they've proved it and more. The Giants, as well, can be proud, having forced a superior eleven beyond the confines of the sixty-minute game before tasting defeat. It's just a shame that Charlie Conerly didn't get to keep that sports car.

SCORING

COLTS	0	14	0	3	6 — 23
GIANTS	3	0	7	7	0 — 17

N.Y.: Summerall, FG, 36.
Bal.: Ameche, 2, run (Myhra, kick).
Bal.: Berry, 15, pass from Unitas (Myhra, kick).
N.Y.: Triplett, 1, run (Summerall, kick).
N.Y.: Gifford, 15, pass from Conerly (Summerall, kick).
Bal.: Myhra, FG, 20.
Bal.: Ameche, 1, run (PAT not attempted).

TEAM STATISTICS

	Colts	Giants
First downs	27	10
Rushing yardage	137	88
Passing yardage	314	179
Punt return yardage	17	8
Passes	24-38	12-18
Interceptions by	0	1
Punts	4-51	6-46
Fumbles lost	2	4
Yards penalized	15	22

INDIVIDUAL STATISTICS

RUSHES—Bal.: Ameche, 15 for 56 yards; Dupre, 11 for 29; Moore, 9 for 24; Unitas, 4 for 28. N.Y.: Gifford, 12 for 60; Webster, 9 for 24; Triplett, 5 for 12; King, 3 for —13; Conerly, 2 for 5.
PASSES—Bal.: Unitas, 24 of 38 for 348 yards. N.Y.: Heinrich, 2 of 4 for 13; Conerly, 10 of 14 for 188.
RECEPTIONS—Bal.: Berry, 12 for 178 yards; Moore, 5 for 99; Mutscheller, 3 for 46; Ameche, 2 for 18; Dupre, 2 for 7. N.Y.: Gifford, 3 for 15 yards; Rote, 2 for 76; Schnelker, 2 for 63; Webster, 2 for 17; Triplett, 2 for 15; McAfee, 1 for 15.

December 26, 1965

BALTIMORE COLTS

VS.

GREEN BAY PACKERS

In the years since that epic overtime clash, Johnny Unitas's reputation for unwavering brilliance tended to obscure the abilities of his teammates: If the Colts won, it was said they won because Unitas was brilliant; if they lost, it was said they lost despite his brilliance. Although the Colts had their share of ups and downs in the years following the sudden-death shootout— costing Weeb Ewbank his job in 1964—they were never a one-man team. They proved that this season, especially last Saturday when they won a game they had no right to win, forcing today's playoff for the Western Conference Championship at Green Bay's Lambeau Field.

The Colts and the Packers are two super teams. One or the other has topped this conference in six of the last seven years, and this year they *both* did. For the Packers, who whipped the Colts twice while scoring 62 points, the deadlock was a disappointment: they could have won the race outright had they not allowed a final-day, final-minute scoring pass by San Francisco's John Brodie. Baltimore, on the other hand, made it here today by concluding its season with a 20–17 victory over the last-place Rams that was one of the proudest moments in the history of the franchise.

The win was unexpected because Johnny Unitas, who had been enjoying another routinely spectacular campaign, went down in the twelfth game with a fractured kneecap. Then, in the very next game, backup Gary Cuozzo suffered a separated shoulder while his team was rudely bumped from first place by the Packers. The Colts employed no third-string quarterback, so halfback Tom Matte finished up, completing none of his three pass attempts. Who would call signals in the fourteenth and final game, which Baltimore had to win? The twenty-six-year-old Matte had been a quarterback at Ohio State, but his coach there, Woody Hayes, didn't care for quarterbacks who threw, so Matte seldom did. Still, Baltimore coach Don Shula reasoned, Matte at least knew the plays (unlike defensive back Bobby Boyd, who also had been a collegiate signal-caller), and thus might be able to manage an offense tailored to his own running ability. The timing of the intricate pass routes on which Unitas and his receivers had worked for years could not be conveyed to Matte in one week's practice sessions, so Shula eliminated the deep routes and simplified the short ones.

With the coaches calling most of the plays from the bench, and Matte supplying the others from a list taped to his left wrist, the Colts hammered out yardage conservatively but effectively. Though Matte attempted only two passes and completed neither, he did run for ninety-nine yards in sixteen carries, mostly on rollouts and draws. In the final minutes he drove his team eighty-

Tom Matte is a decidedly unflashy running back who simply gets the job done. But can he do the job as an emergency quarterback? There's precedent—in 1952 the Giants lost their two quarterbacks to injury in the same contest, and a defensive back named Tom Landry (whom we'll meet in the next chapter) took over for a couple of games and nearly led his team to the conference championship.

five yards in thirteen plays to position the winning field goal.

Last week's heroics aside, the question to be answered on this damp, breezy, chilly afternoon is: If the Colts were only able to beat the last-place Rams by three points, how can they hope to keep pace with the Packers?

Shula's game plan will be essentially the same as it was last week: to remove as much risk as possible from his offense through simple play selection, and to shift that allowance for risk to the defense, permitting them to stunt and blitz and swarm, trying to create turnovers. Packer coach Vince Lombardi's game plan will be to adjust to Baltimore's strengths: playing the secondary closer to the line to deny Matte short flips to the backs, and having the Packer ends pinch off the outside to thwart the rollout. On offense Lombardi has inserted some rollout plays for his own quarterback, Bart Starr, to frustrate the anticipated Baltimore blitz.

Vince Lombardi served as an assistant coach in New York from 1954 through 1958—the sudden-death game was his last as a Giant—then was hired as head coach by woeful Green Bay. In his first year at the helm, he took essentially the same squad that had gone 1-10-1 the previous year and motivated them to a record of 7–5. He led them to the title game in 1960, and to the top of the heap the next two years, whipping a very good Giant team in the championship contest both times. His gruff emphasis on discipline, pride, and preparedness rankled some of his players, but most of the Packers, big-hearted as only winners can be, came around to the point of view expressed by defensive tackle Henry Jordan: "He's fair. He treats us all the same—like dogs."

Shula also runs a tight ship, modeled in large part on the methods and rigor of Cleveland's Paul Brown, under whom Shula broke into the NFL as a defensive back in the 1950s. When Weeb Ewbank, also a Brown disciple, stopped winning championships with his easygoing manner, Colts' owner Carroll

Rosenbloom, seeing Lombardi's success in Green Bay, canned Weeb and hired the taskmaster Shula. After only one year of transition Shula restored the Colts to their former heights, easing in new talent as some of the older stars began to dim. So today, we will revisit several of the Colts whose acquaintance we made in 1958, and be introduced to many new ones.

Set to kick off for Baltimore is Lou Michaels, a left-footer who also starts at left end now that Gino Marchetti has retired to run his fast-food restaurant business. Lou blasts the ball six yards into the end zone, where Tom Moore fields it, hesitates, then decides to bring it out. The Colts bury him at the 15, and out comes the Packer offensive unit.

Bart Starr takes the snap and drops back to pass, a surprise call to open the game. He spots tight end Bill Anderson crossing from right to left and hits him at the 25. But when Anderson is drilled from behind by cornerback Lenny Lyles, the ball pops free! Linebacker Don Shinnick, who had been trailing the play, scoops it up and races for the right corner of the end zone. Starr seems to have an angle on him at the 5. He crouches, trying to spill cornerback Jim Welch, who is leading Shinnick's interference, and allow another Packer to make the tackle. But in silent-movie slapstick style, Starr and Welch and Shinnick collide, their bodies entangling, then flying off in different directions. Shinnick stays on his feet and continues into the end zone, waving the ball in triumph. Starr gets up slowly, his hand to his rib cage. And up at the 25-yard line, Anderson is also slow to rise, still woozy from Lyles's crunching tackle; though he will play the rest of the game, he will not remember any of it.

Only thirty-one seconds after his opening kickoff, with the ticketholders just settling into their seats, Michaels blasts off the tee again. Herb Adderley gets out only as far as the 18, where Green Bay's offense will take over—without Starr, who is gamely trying to throw on the sidelines despite a painful muscle tear. At the helm for the moment is thirty-three-year-old Zeke Bratkowski, a starter with the Bears and the Rams in previous years who has seen very little action in his two seasons as Starr's understudy. Losing Starr for the entire game would be a terrible blow to the Packers; but, keeping things in perspective, Bratkowski is a professional quarterback of demonstrated ability, unlike Matte.

On first down Paul Hornung runs for seven. Green Bay's "Golden Boy" since 1960, when he set a single-season (only twelve games) scoring mark of 176 points that may never be equaled, he was tarnished when the league cited him for gambling and suspended him for the entire 1963 season. When he returned the following year he seemed to have lost his former verve. Then, two weeks ago against the Colts, Paul scored five touchdowns to give his fans hope that he was, at last, all the way back.

Hornung's less glamorous but even more productive running mate is Jim Taylor, a power hitter from the old school who would be recognized as the best fullback in the game today were it not for Jim Brown. Taylor lowers his shoulder and barrels into the line on the next two plays, picking up the first down. Then, following a pass to Anderson for eight, Hornung circles left end for seven more, to the Packer 45. Next, Hornung knifes through the line for three, but as he brushes a Colt lineman the ball squirts forward to midfield, where Lyles recovers for Baltimore.

The fans are fidgety. This kind of sloppiness was supposed to have disappeared with the advent of Lombardi. But the worried hum of the stadium turns into a joyous shout as Baltimore, on its first play from scrimmage, returns the favor. Lenny Moore, taking the handoff from Matte and heading off right tackle, is really popped at the line and loses the ball. Safety Tom Brown, who two summers ago played first base with the Washington Senators, fields the ball at the line of scrimmage.

While Starr continues to lob passes weakly on the sidelines,

Hornung and Taylor come up one yard short of the first down. Don Chandler—whom the Giants foolishly peddled to the Packers this year—comes on to try a forty-eight-yard field goal. Starr is in to hold. This will, it develops, be the only duty he is able to perform today. In the years since we saw Chandler last, he has become a fine placekicker as well as a great punter—but his attempt falls short.

The remainder of the first quarter is taken up with a punting duel between Chandler and Baltimore's Tom Gilburg. The defenses utterly dominate: In five possessions, neither team can gain so much as a first down. The Packers' cause is not helped by two consecutive dropped passes by Taylor, and Baltimore is hindered by the fact that split end Raymond Berry and flanker Jimmy Orr are just going through the motions—they might as well have their hands tied behind them for all the passes they will catch today. Matte does complete one toss in the quarter—his first as a pro quarterback—to tight end John Mackey for a mere six yards.

Shula, having seen his wide-running attack of the first quarter yield a puny seventeen yards on eight carries, now realizes that Green Bay's spread-out defensive alignment will turn in any venture to the outside. Every defense gives you something, he knows, and he sends in plays with which Matte can probe the middle. On first down from the Colt 25, Hill cracks over center for four. Matte drops back, pauses, then bursts up the middle on a draw for four more; a late hit on the play gives the Colts an additional fifteen yards.

Hill rushes twice for four yards, then on third down the Packers look for a dump over the middle to Mackey. Matte fades, dropping deeper as the Packer linemen beat their blockers; but the breakdown in pass protection is intentional—Matte flips a screen pass over the onrushing linemen to Moore for nine yards and a first down at the Packer 39. Returning to the ground game between the tackles, Hill, Matte, and Moore peel off yardage in good-sized chunks down to the 8. On third down, however, reserve fullback Tony Lorick is stopped. Michaels boots the easy fifteen-yard field goal, and the surprising Colts lead ten–zip.

With only five minutes left in the half, the fans beseech their Packers to show some life. If only Starr were in there, many of them think. Bratkowski looks to his flanker, Caroll Dale, for the first time in the game, and connects for a first down. A flip to Hornung produces another first, on Green Bay's 44. The line is giving Zeke plenty of time to pick out his receivers, so he cranks up again. Looking for Bob Long, who has just come in at flanker for Dale, Bratkowski heaves the ball some fifty-five yards in the air, but incomplete. No—wait . . . it's ruled interference against safety Jerry Logan! The Packers get the ball on the Baltimore 9.

Throwing again on first down, Bratkowski fires to Anderson at the right sideline; he struggles to within one foot of the goal. Now Baltimore shifts into a 5-1 defense, something the Packers haven't seen in their two previous meetings with Baltimore. The extra down-lineman disrupts the offensive line's blocks, and Taylor's dive is thrown back for no gain. Hornung also fails on third down, and Lombardi is confronted with a decision. He wants to get on the scoreboard before halftime, yet he doesn't want to give Baltimore the moral victory of his settling for three points only inches short of the goal. He keeps his kicking team on the sidelines, to the delight of the fans.

Bratkowski hands to Taylor, who veers right and darts in, only to be hit from the side by Michaels. Taylor bounces off and spins back toward the middle, where he is zapped by middle linebacker Dennis Gaubatz. The ball falls to earth, then hops back into the fallen Taylor's arms—still inches shy of the end zone.

The Colts have held, but they are not yet out of hot water. There is still 1:40 to play, and they must achieve a first down or give Green Bay field position for at least a field-goal attempt. On first down Matte sneaks for no gain, barely making it out of the end zone. Then the Baltimore offensive line hitches up its pants and gets to work. Matte hits for six, then six again for the vital first down. Matte for five. Matte for two—and Green Bay can only watch the seconds tick off on the first half of this upset in the making.

To this point the story of the game has been defense (remember, the Colts' offense had nothing to do with their touchdown). These kinds of battles in the pits are a football purist's delight—lots of hitting, with every yard a tough one and each scoring opportunity critical. Watching a defensive battle is like watching a pitchers' duel in baseball—the seeming inaction of the game becomes its action, until the rhythm is abruptly and stirringly broken.

Chandler's second-half kickoff hits the crossbar for a touchback. Baltimore comes out doing the same things that worked so well at the end of the first half. Hill churns for two, Matte passes to Moore in the flat for six, and Moore rushes for the first down. But the Colts stall at their 40, and Gilburg comes on to punt. Disaster—Buzz Nutter's snap is high! Gilburg leaps, bobbles the ball, drops it, and then picks it up. By this time the Colt line can hold out the rush no longer. As the Packers break through, Gilburg tries to scramble for the first down, but is tackled at his 35.

The Packers must capitalize on this break. Taylor gains one as the impatient crowd boos: Starr would never have made such a call! Bratkowski sends Dale downfield on a crossing pattern, waits calmly in the pocket as Dale is tripped while trying to break free, then hits him for a big gain to the 1. Redemption. The Colts realign into the 5-1 that saved a score earlier. At halftime, however, the Packers discussed how they would adjust their blocking in this spot, and now they do it. Hornung goes over easily behind Jerry Kramer, Chandler adds the point, and the Pack is back: 10–7.

As so often happens when a frustrated team finally scores, its

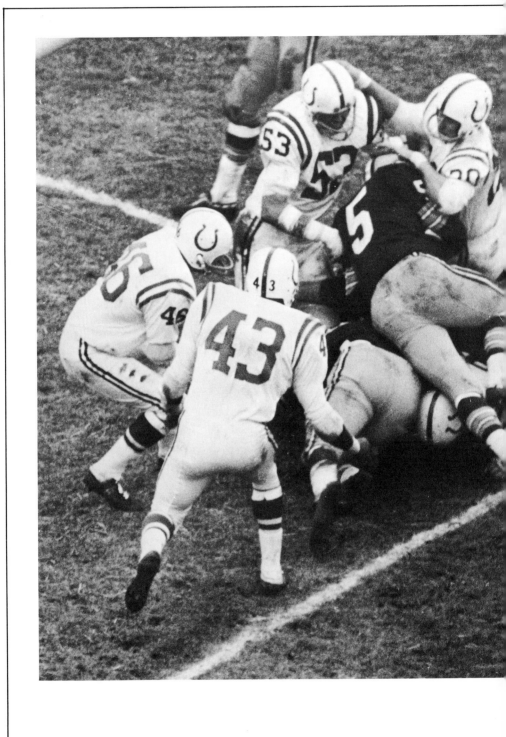

Jerry Kramer and Forrest Gregg bury the Colts' linemen, and Paul Hornung (5) vaults over from the 1. Now each team has notched a touchdown following an opposition blunder.

defense is pumped up and gets the ball right back. Regaining possession at the Packer 17, Bratkowski finds Hornung for a nineteen-yard completion. On third and two from the 44, he passes to Anderson over the middle for another first down. This simple slant-in has been open all game long because middle linebacker Gaubatz is concentrating on the run, and is overly susceptible to the play-action fake. Besides, the Colts have yet to pick up on Green Bay's tactic of throwing on first down: seven pass attempts on first down have produced five completions and that big interference call. Maybe I spoke too soon: On first and fifteen following a motion penalty, safety Bobby Boyd snatches a deep pass intended for split end Boyd Dowler.

The Packers' defense has lately begun to seal off the middle as well as the ends, pulling in the secondary even tighter and virtually daring Matte to throw a medium-range pass. On third and five Matte does go to Berry on the left side, but the play doesn't click. Gilburg punts yet again.

Chandler, too, must kick the ball away on the next series, for Bratkowski's third-down pass to Dowler is two yards short of the first down. But as he punts from his 45 to open the fourth quarter, the Colts charge offside, providing Green Bay with a gift first down. A team under as much pressure as Baltimore right now can ill afford such blunders.

A sideliner to Dowler brings up a third and three from the Baltimore 43, which Bratkowski converts with a ten-yard pass to Hornung. Paul then runs a power sweep right, with guards Jerry Kramer and Fuzzy Thurston pulling out of the line to block, and picks up eight more (see diagram). Taylor follows with a four-yard gain for a first down at the 21. The fans sense a score. Bratkowski has riddled Baltimore's vaunted zone defense, with the aid of his outstanding protection, and now the run has opened up too. He pitches to Hornung again, who sweeps right, then stops—it's a pass! Just as Lombardi made the halfback option a feared play with Frank Gifford, so has he shaken up

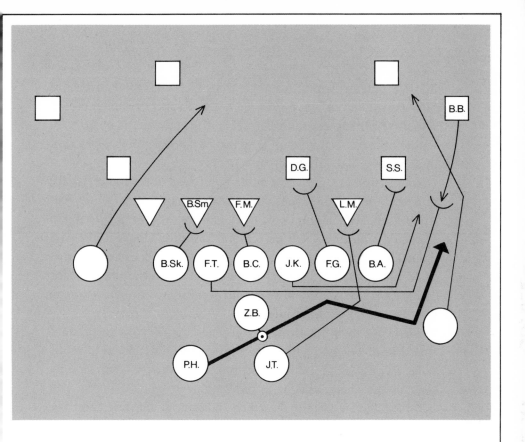

Vince Lombardi's power sweep was inspired by the old single wing, in which a pulling guard led the interference. In the Green Bay version, however, two guards pull out of the line—whence the "power." Paul Hornung (P.H.) takes the handoff from Zeke Bratkowski (Z.B.), continues toward the line, then "bellies back" to make way for Fuzzy Thurston (F.T.) and Jerry Kramer (J.K.), whom he will follow around end. Bob Skoronski (B.Sk.) ignores the defensive right end and blocks Thurston's man, Billy Ray Smith (B.Sm.). On the other side of the line, Forrest Gregg (F.G.) covers for Kramer by taking out Dennis Gaubatz (D.G.). This allows Lou Michaels (L.M.) to penetrate, but fullback Jim Taylor (J.T.) picks him off. Center Bill Curry (B.C.) fires straight out at Fred Miller (F.M.), and tight end Bill Anderson (B.A.) cuts down Steve Stonebreaker (S.S.). As Hornung breaks past the line, Thurston targets cornerback Bobby Boyd (B.B.), while Kramer freelances.

many a defense with Hornung (who, like Gifford, had been a quarterback in college). But here the Packer fortunes take a tumble. Hornung's pass to Dowler in the end zone is broken up, and Bratkowski's follow-up is tipped at the line, then picked off by Jerry Logan to kill the drive.

Can Baltimore protect a three-point lead for another twelve minutes? Only if the offense can generate something. Matte tries to do it himself, but on two carries gains a total of one yard. On third and nine, he rolls to the left and looks for Mackey. The pass connects for sixteen yards, an important gain because it allows the Colt defenders another minute and a half of rest. When Matte's pass on third and five is no good, they are ready to man their battle stations once more.

From his own 28, Bratkowski mixes up his calls to produce two first downs and place the ball squarely at midfield. As he fades to pass on first down his protection collapses, for the first time in the game, and he is barely able to get rid of the ball before Billy Ray Smith hammers a right to his jaw. For this undue bit of rowdiness Billy Ray is slapped with a penalty, putting the Packers on Baltimore's 43. From there Bratkowski continues to pick and peck: a pass to Anderson for six, a run by Taylor for four, another pass to Anderson for fourteen.

Just over two minutes remain to be played when a third-down pass to Taylor fails. Don Chandler comes on to try a tying 3-pointer from a sharp angle at the 22.

Bill Curry snaps, Starr holds, and Chandler steps into the ball. As the kick sails high over the left goalpost, Chandler shakes his head in disgust and Colts' end Ordell Braase smacks his hands in exultation. Then comes the call from field judge Jim Tunney: "Good!" Some Colts race toward referee Norm Schachter to protest the call—they are certain the ball sailed outside the invisible plane of the goalpost. But the argument is over before it begins; there is no reversing such a call. In future years the goalposts will be raised to twenty feet above the crossbar to make

*Out of camera range, the Colts' Ordell Braase wraps his arms around
Zeke Bratkowski's legs. As Zeke falls forward he dumps the ball to
avoid the loss, but he cannot avoid the charge of Billy Ray Smith, who
comes in late and irate. Yellow flag; fifteen yards.*

the field judge's call less tricky, but on this day we are tied: 10–10.

Alvin Haymond returns Chandler's kickoff to the 22, and the Colts take over with 1:40 to play—plenty of time for a Unitas to bring his team into field-goal range with a flurry of crisp sideline passes, but for Matte an impossibility. Once his first-down attempt to Berry falls incomplete, he resolves to kill as much of the clock as possible, keeping the ball on the ground. Shula has instructed him not to risk an interception on a low-percentage pass, but rather to trust to Providence and the Colt defense in overtime.

When Gilburg's punt is returned to the 38, only twenty-seven seconds remain. The Packers want to win this thing now—anything can happen in sudden death. With everyone covered downfield, Bratkowski swings a pass out to Tom Moore, who accepts a loss of four in order to get out of bounds; the Packers have used up their allotted timeouts. Next Zeke combines with Taylor for a twenty-yard gain to the Baltimore 46, but Jim cannot get out of bounds. As the clock winds down, the kicking team races onto the field for a fifty-three-yard attempt.

They are too late. We are going to overtime, for the second time in NFL postseason history.

Green Bay wins the toss, but does nothing with its crucial opening possession. Alvin Haymond returns Chandler's punt to his own 41, setting the Colts up in excellent field position. But Matte is no more successful than Bratkowski, misfiring on two passes just as Zeke did.

Green Bay gets another shot (which is more than Johnny Unitas gave the Giants). A pass to Taylor in the flat is good for nine to the Packer 30. On second and one Bratkowski goes for broke, looking deep after a play-action fake—but the fake fools no one, the receivers are blanketed, and Zeke is thrown for a loss of eight. His third-down pass to Moore swinging out of the backfield fails, and the Colts again get the ball on their 41 following Chandler's kick.

The two defenses, each asked to contribute more in support of a crippled offense, have given everything they have to give. Only two weeks ago these same teams—except for the quarterbacks—raced up and down the field to a final score of 42–27!

On first down Matte steps back as if to pass, then scurries for nine yards between left defensive end Willie Davis and left tackle Ron Kostelnik. The offensive right tackle, George Preas, offered the outside pass-rush route to Davis, and Davis took himself out of the play. On second down Matte comes back with the identical quarterback draw, and it works for five yards and a first down. And *again*—Matte for eight to the Green Bay 37! Tom has been hero enough simply to bring his team to this game and keep them in it—is it possible that he can win?

In the defensive huddle Davis, embarrassed and angry, changes the defensive alignment on his own, without consulting the coaching staff. He decides to play Preas head-on, leaving the outside responsibility to middle linebacker Ray Nitschke. And it works—Lenny Moore is thrown for a loss of one, and Matte's next quarterback draw loses two. Still, the Colts have been pushed back only as far as the 40, not too far out for the powerful left leg of Lou Michaels.

Boyd kneels at the 47, awaiting the snap. As Nutter releases the ball, Michaels steps forward, then halts as the snap bounces. Boyd short-hops the football, then hurriedly places it down. But by this time Michaels's timing has been destroyed, and he puts his foot to the ball awkwardly and weakly. The kick is short. Green Bay takes over at the 20.

Their nerves frayed to the snapping point, the fans implore their heroes to ease their suffering. Elijah Pitts, in the game at halfback because Hornung twisted his knee in the last series, gains four off tackle. Now Bratkowski looks to Anderson, on the slant that has worked time and again. It clicks for eighteen yards. For Bill Anderson, who came out of retirement to join the Packers this year, that is his eighth catch of the day—as many as he'd caught in the entire regular season!

Hitting the hole between tackle and end again, Pitts gains six and Taylor five. Another first down. Then Taylor for three. And now Bratkowski goes up top: flankerback Dale races downfield, splits the seam in the zone, turns to the sideline, leaps . . . and catches the ball, just barely landing in bounds at the 26.

That'll be the last pass Zeke throws today. He is in field-goal range right now, and the next three downs are only to make Chandler's position ideal. On fourth and two from the 18, the kicking team comes on. Curry snaps the ball back to Starr at the 25, and, peering through a tangle of upraised Colt arms, Chandler boots the ball cleanly between the uprights. There's no doubt about this one. After thirteen minutes and thirty-three seconds of the overtime period—making this the longest NFL game ever played up to this time—the Packers have won 13–10.

In tomorrow's newspapers, and in other accounts through the years, observers will give grudging credit to the Packers (whose offensive heroes, Bratkowski and Chandler, were in truth not exceptional), while acclaiming Matte as the true hero of the game. Matte's quarterbacking was, as Samuel Johnson said of a dog that walked on its hind legs, "not done well; but you are surprised to find it done at all."

The real stars of this not-so-sudden-death classic are the undeservedly anonymous defenders on both sides, but especially those of Baltimore. Not only did they press a superior team beyond the limits of regulation play, they scored their club's only touchdown. Whoever first said that defense is the name of the game could not have imagined a finer performance.

SCORING

COLTS	7	3	0	0	0 — 10
PACKERS	0	0	7	3	3 — 13

Bal.: Shinnick, 25, fumble return (Michaels, kick).
Bal.: Michaels, FG, 15.
G.B.: Hornung, 1, run (Chandler, kick).
G.B.: Chandler, FG, 27.
G.B.: Chandler, FG, 25.

TEAM STATISTICS

	Colts	Packers
First downs	9	23
Rushing yardage	143	112
Passing yardage	32	250
Punt return yardage	21	17
Passes	5-12	23-41
Interceptions by	2	0
Punts	8-41	5-43
Fumbles lost	1	2
Yards penalized	59	40

INDIVIDUAL STATISTICS

RUSHES—Bal.: Matte, 17 for 57 yards; Hill, 16 for 57; Moore, 12 for 33; Lorick, 1 for 1; Gilburg, 1 for —5. G.B.: Taylor, 23 for 60; Hornung, 10 for 33; Pitts, 3 for 14; Moore, 3 for 5.

PASSES—Bal.: Matte, 5 of 12 for 40 yards. G.B.: Bratkowski, 22 of 39 for 248; Starr, 1 of 1 for 10; Hornung, 0 for 1.

RECEPTIONS—Bal.: Mackey, 3 for 25 yards; Moore, 2 for 15. G.B.: Anderson, 8 for 78; Dowler, 5 for 50; Dale, 3 for 63; Hornung, 4 for 42; Taylor, 2 for 29; Moore, 1 for —4.

January 1, 1967

GREEN BAY PACKERS
VS.
DALLAS COWBOYS

The year after Vince Lombardi left the Giants' coaching staff to head a crumbling operation in Green Bay, Tom Landry also left New York to take on an even bigger challenge in Dallas. Lombardi took over a team that had won only one game in 1958, but he did inherit much of the talent that would soon propel Green Bay to the heights: Jerry Kramer, Ray Nitschke, Forrest Gregg, Jesse Whittenton, Bill Forester, Dan Currie, Jim Ringo, Paul Hornung, Bart Starr, Jim Taylor—*each one of them a future all-pro.* Landry, however, assumed control of an expansion franchise that had no players, that would be stocked through the college draft and a rummage sale of the other clubs' undesirables. Not surprisingly, where Lombardi in his first season

82

was able to work a miracle and post a record of 7–5, Landry's inaugural campaign in 1960 produced eleven losses, one tie, and no victories.

And yet Landry has proven to be a miracle worker as well. By 1962, his third year at the helm, the undermanned Cowboys somehow generated pro football's second-best offense. By 1964, they pulled together its fourth-best defense. And by 1966, they topped the Eastern Conference, earning the right to battle the defending-champion Packers for the NFL title on this sunny New Year's Day in Dallas.

The Cotton Bowl is filled today with nearly 75,000 devoted Cowboy fans; yet only fifteen years ago the Dallas Texans couldn't draw flies in this town, and were forced to hit the road for good after only four home dates. It's ironic that those nomadic Texans became the Baltimore Colts, whose overtime victory in 1958 promoted so much interest in pro football that an expansion into Dallas was deemed possible.

A further irony of this irresistible matchup—the number-one defense in the Packers, the number-one offense in the Cowboys —is that when they were both assistant coaches with the Giants, it was Lombardi who ran the team's offense while Landry handled the defense! What's more, Landry can be said to have invented the 4-3 defense which every pro team used this year. He modified Steve Owen's umbrella defense (a 6-1) by dropping two men off the line to become linebackers, thus leaving the front four to defend the middle while trusting that speedy pursuit by the linebackers would contain the sweeps.

As the architect of that defense, Landry, once he became a head coach, contrived to destroy it, through an abruptly shifting "multiple offense" of exotic formations. In this, too, as with the 4-3 defense, Landry stood on the shoulders of a Giant: coach Owen, who in 1952 wrote that his dream was to employ an ever-shifting offense, one that could "go from A to T to double wing to southwest spread from play to play. I could put unprecedented pressure on defenses, particularly since many teams cannot handle several formations without changing personnel. Whether the Giants or some other team achieves it first, it is the coming thing in football." Owen hoped to achieve a multiple offense with Frank Gifford as his all-purpose tailback, but that never came to be. Landry's version employs spreads and slots and men in motion and double wings and the shotgun, and this year, led by quarterback Don Meredith, it put 32 points a game on the scoreboard.

The Packers, on the other hand, don't try to confuse the opposition so much as they aim to outhit and outexecute it, which they do with such regularity that they are the undisputed cream of the league. This year, without being fancy, they lost only two games, by a total of 4 points. In fact, in preparation for today's game, Lombardi has pared down his entire playbook to six passing plays, with variations, and eight runs. He has discarded his best running play, the power sweep, in acknowledgment of the Cowboys' excellent pursuit from their "flex" defense, in which a tackle on one side of the line and an end on the other side play a foot or two off the ball, the better to hem in a wide run. Lombardi's other adjustments to the flex have been to install new blocking assignments for the inside runs and to cross his backs, hoping to freeze the linebackers for a critical split second.

It's three o'clock, showtime, and the Cowboys' Danny Villanueva kicks off to Donny Anderson, one of two high-priced, little-used rookies (the other is fullback Jim Grabowski) whom the Packers are grooming to replace the aging tandem of Hornung and Taylor. Anderson returns to the 24 and the offensive unit trots on.

Quarterback Bart Starr hands the ball to Elijah Pitts, who has started most of the year in place of the injured Hornung. After crossing with Taylor, Pitts cracks between the blocks of

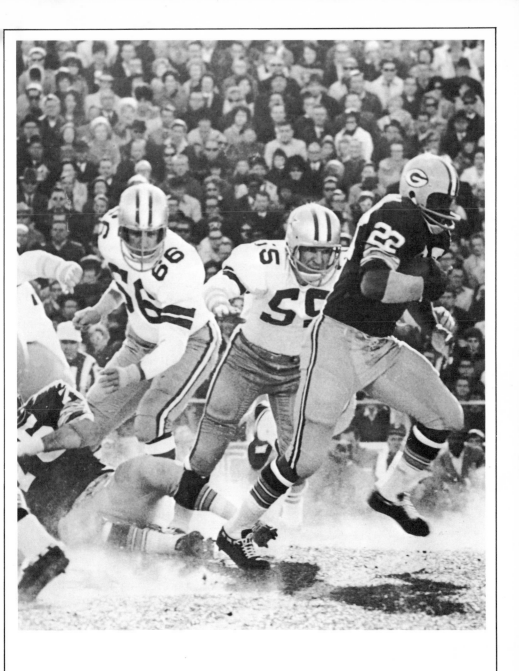

Although Elijah Pitts (22) played well this year as a replacement for the injured Paul Hornung, pregame speculation was that Vince Lombardi would return the starting spot to Green Bay's Golden Boy. Not so. On the first play from scrimmage, Pitts rewards his coach's confidence in him, breaking away for a thirty-two-yard gain.

right tackle Forrest Gregg and tight end Marv Fleming and breaks into the secondary; Mel Renfro races to make the tackle, but only after Pitts has gained thirty-two yards to the Dallas 44.

Starr hits Dale for nine, then gives to Taylor for the first down. After Bob Lilly bats down a pass at the line and then slams Taylor for a three-yard loss on a flare pass, the Cowboy fans begin whooping it up. But a third-down toss to Dale keeps the drive going, and two plays later Pitts takes a swing pass from the 17, eludes three tacklers, and weaves his way in for the score. Don Chandler converts the PAT, and Green Bay has jumped out to a 7–0 lead with disturbing ease. Indeed, the packed Cotton Bowl is now as silent as it must have been for the Dallas Texans.

In an instant, the fans' concern is transformed into despair. Taking Chandler's kickoff at the goal line, Renfro zips forward to the 18. There he is sandwiched by Gale Gillingham and Bob Brown, whose combined weight is some 520 pounds. He fumbles. The football takes one bounce, then just lies there on the ground for an agonizing second before Jim Grabowski comes along, scoops it up, and rambles into the end zone untouched. The game is four minutes and thirty-one seconds old, the Dallas offense has yet to touch the ball, and the score is 14–0.

What we have here is a test of character. Not only is this the Cowboys' first NFL championship game, it also caps their first winning season; you could hardly blame them if they panicked now and started bombing to get back in the game. But Landry will not let his young team lose its composure—he knows that to stray from the game plan at this early juncture would be the road to ruin.

Taking over at their 35 after Renfro's return of the kickoff, the Cowboys keep the ball on the ground to get the feel of the game and to slow down its pace. Dandy Don Meredith, one of four original Cowboys on this squad, hands to halfback Dan Reeves for four yards off tackle. (These two, along with split end

Bob Hayes and fullback Don Perkins, have been the prime movers of the Dallas offense: Meredith threw twenty-four touchdown passes while mastering the complexities of the multiple offense, and Reeves ran for eight scores while catching passes for eight more.) Perkins, the undersized fullback of uncommon quickness, bursts up the middle for seven. Reeves comes back off left tackle for four. The Cowboys have hit the left, the right, and the middle of the Packer line and found worthwhile yardage each time.

Continuing to strut out new stuff, Meredith hits flanker Pete Gent for seven, then goes to a little razzle-dazzle: an end-around, with tight end Pettis Norman circling back for six. Dallas is on the Packer 43 and rolling. Reeves takes a pitchout and sweeps the right side for three. On third down and one Bob Hayes, "the world's fastest human" (he has run a 9.1 100-yard dash), the most feared end in the game, is the intended receiver, but cornerback Herb Adderley knocks the pass away.

The busted gamble brings up a fourth down at the 34. The stadium reverberates with cheers as Landry allows his offense to go for the first—and Reeves makes it, with three yards to spare. Now Meredith fires into the flat for Hayes, a potential long-gainer if he can get a block on the cornerback—but Bullet Bob fumbles after taking a step, and falls on the ball for a paltry gain of one.

Now Meredith hits Gent for eleven yards and, after Reeves is stopped for no gain, Norman for twelve. A personal foul moves the ball to the Packer 3. From this point Reeves walks through a gaping hole off right tackle into the end zone. Sixty-five yards in thirteen plays: this impressive drive signals the Packers that they are in for a ball game after all.

Urged on by the crowd, the defense rises up and asserts itself, too. Anderson is allowed to bring the kickoff back only to the 13. Middle linebacker Lee Roy Jordan—a roving destroyer in the mold of Landry's earlier star, Sam Huff—fills the gap off left tackle to stop Pitts for no gain. Starr throws for Boyd Dowler, incomplete, then is nailed by right end George Andrie for a loss of seven.

That old devil momentum is squarely with Dallas now. Taking over on their 41 after a fine Chandler punt, the Cowboys move into Green Bay territory on two rushes by Perkins. A pass to Reeves, who is covered only by a linebacker, connects for twenty-two. Then on second and eleven from the 23, Perkins squirts through a hole off right guard, eludes two tacklers, and bursts into the clear for the touchdown! The point is good, and with thirty-six seconds remaining in this action-packed first quarter, accounts are squared at 14 all.

Never before in championship play has each team scored two touchdowns in a quarter. And these are two of the stingiest outfits in football—the Cowboys were tops against the run this year and the Packers were best against the pass. When will these fine defenses exert some control?

Not yet, anyway. After an offside penalty moves the ball to the Packer 49 on the opening play of the period, Starr goes downtown to Carroll Dale, who has a step on cornerback Cornell Green. The ball is underthrown, however, allowing Green to close the distance between himself and Dale. Sensing that the pass is ripe for interception, Green leaps—but prematurely. The ball drops into Dale's waiting arms. Twenty-one to fourteen! The purists may be groaning, but everyone else is in a frenzy of excitement.

From the 28-yard line, the Cowboys renew their attack. And propelled by Reeves's five rushes and forty-yard catch, they drive inside the Green Bay 10-yard line, where Landry replaces Hayes with Frank Clarke, a superior blocker. On third and goal from the 4, Meredith hits Clarke, but beyond the end zone. Villanueva comes on to boot the easy field goal, and the score is 21–17. Thus far only one possession has failed to produce a score!

And the fireworks continue. On first down from the 22, Pitts charges off left tackle for twenty-four yards. Passes to Fleming and Taylor push the ball to the Dallas 25. But on third and eight, the drive stops as Pitts drops a pass and Chandler's thirty-yard field-goal try is deflected by Ralph Neely. The superheated offenses seem to take this as their cue to simmer down till the second half. An exchange of punts follows, after which the Cowboys, hemmed in deep in their own end, run out the clock. Enough action for you?

On the opening series of the second half, the Packers are able to stop the Cowboys thanks to linebacker Dave Robinson's fine third-down tackle of Pettis Norman, one yard short of the first. Bart Starr, the 1956 seventeenth-round draft choice who was the league's top quarterback this year, sets out to widen his team's 4-point advantage. On third and nine at the Packer 31, he finds Dowler at the left sideline for ten. On third and seven at his 44, he hits Dale for eleven. Starr's ability to convert third downs in obvious passing situations is a special gift, one of the things that make him an exceptional quarterback.

Another pass, to reserve receiver Bob Long, is sandwiched between two fine Taylor runs. But at the Dallas 23, Pitts is whacked by linebacker Chuck Howley and fumbles; cornerback Warren Livingston recovers.

Now Dallas mounts a drive, with Meredith converting two third-and-long situations of his own. But as the Cowboys advance into Green Bay territory, Bob Hayes continues to be invisible, dropping one pass and seeing another whiz by him. To this point five passes have been directed his way and only one has been completed, for a gain of one yard. Hayes is contributing to the offense, nonetheless; as a decoy on nearly every pass play, he continues to receive double coverage deep.

After completing a pass to Reeves at the 37, Dandy Don catches the Packers by surprise with a rollout around right end

When Lombardi took over the Packers in 1959, Bart Starr was one of four quarterbacks who stood a chance of being a preseason cut from a team that had gone 1-10-1. In 1977, Starr entered the Hall of Fame.

for eleven. But the Cowboys can only move one yard on their next three plays, and from the 32 Villanueva boots another field goal. Dallas has drawn within one point of the mighty Packers; for the underdog expansion team, victory is within reach.

Seeming to toy with Dallas, Starr takes only five plays to pull his team further out in front. On first down from his 26, Bart once again finds that Dale has beaten Green downfield and connects for forty-three yards. A four-yard dive by Taylor, a five-yard pass to Taylor, a penalty, and a one-yard run by Pitts position the Packers at the Dallas 16. Starr fades, then fakes a draw to Taylor, pulling middle linebacker Jordan in a few steps. Taylor carries out the fake past the line, then cuts right as if to receive a pass, taking left linebacker Howley with him. Meanwhile, from his split-end spot Boyd Dowler has sped downfield some ten yards, then cut diagonally across the middle toward the end zone. As Dowler nears the seam in the zone between safeties Mel Renfro and Mike Gaechter, Starr has a clear path to throw the ball to him, since Taylor has neatly disposed of the linebackers. The pass is on the money. Dowler makes the catch and tumbles headfirst over Gaechter into the end zone. Chandler's kick makes the score 28–20. Are the Packers playing only as hard as they have to?

The fourth period opens with Dallas on its 35, following a fine return of kickoff by Renfro. Rushes by Meredith and Perkins provide a first down at the 46. Now Meredith goes to the air, but a drop by Gent and two poorly thrown balls force Dallas to kick the ball away.

Villanueva's weak punt gives Green Bay possession on its 26 rather than inside the 10, as he had hoped. And Starr picks up right where he left off, firing to Dowler again, this time for twenty-three yards. But here the Dallas defense draws the line, sacking Starr on third down. Chandler, punting from his 46, gets away a moonshot to the goal line. As the ball descends toward Hayes, Renfro stands beside him yelling to let the ball land in the end zone for a touchback. But the frustrated Hayes is determined to turn on the burners and get his team some field position. Backpedaling into the end zone, he catches the ball, then barely gets out to the 1-yard line before being buried.

Dallas has been pushed up against the wall. They must at least give Villanueva room to punt. Behind right guard Leon Donohue, Perkins slashes through the line for five, then gets three more behind left tackle Jim Boeke. Third and two—a critical call—and the handoff goes to Reeves, who follows left guard Tony Liscio for four yards. But just as they did in their previous series, the Cowboys go to the air after gaining on the ground, and come up empty. Two passes to Gent fail to connect, making seven incompletions in a row for Meredith, then Don is dropped for a loss by Henry Jordan. Punting from his own end zone, Villanueva gets off a high floater; Anderson signals a fair catch at the Dallas 48. For the Cowboys, the game is in danger of slipping away right now—with 9:22 left, they cannot allow even a first down, for a field goal would put them down by 11.

On first down Pitts and Taylor cross, with Pitts taking the handoff on a reverse around left end; but Willie Townes corrals Pitts for a loss of one. As the fans roar with glee, George Andrie bursts through the line to nail Starr for a loss of eight, bringing up a third down and nineteen back at the Packer 43. But this is when Starr is at his most dangerous, as he proves once again with a twenty-four-yard pass over the middle to Fleming.

From the Dallas 33, Starr overthrows Pitts, then slips the ball to Taylor on a delay that fails to fool Townes, who makes the tackle two yards behind the line. Third down and twelve: Starr flips to Taylor for sixteen. The spectators cannot believe what they are seeing. After Taylor gains two yards, Starr fades to throw; but the left side of the ferocious Cowboy front four, who led the league in sacks this season, overpowers the Packer line and throws Starr for another loss, this time eleven yards.

Yet on third and nineteen from the 28 Starr converts *again*—all the way for the score! The recipient of Starr's fourth touchdown pass of the day is Max McGee, a thirty-four-year-old veteran who was used so sparingly this season that he caught only four passes. The Packers lead 34–20 and Dallas's hopes are crushed; few in the disheartened throng care, or even notice, that Chandler's extra-point attempt is blocked by Bob Lilly.

Renfro returns the kickoff to the 29, and Meredith and crew take over with 5:10 to play. A pass to Norman is good for eight, then Meredith picks up the first down with a run of five. After misfiring to reserve Buddy Dial, Meredith completes a screen to Reeves—who fumbles! Fortunately Don, showing no sense of self-preservation, dives for the ball and recovers it; but the Cowboys lose ten yards on the play.

So, on third and twenty from his own 32, needing two touchdowns to win, Meredith must throw deep. As the play begins, Reeves is put in motion to the right, and the linebackers ease over with him—particularly left linebacker Robinson, who thus permits Frank Clarke, the tight end on this play, to get downfield without a chuck at the line. On the right, flanker Pete Gent cuts to the sideline, taking Adderley with him. On the left, Hayes sprints to the inside of cornerback Bob Jeter, then cuts back outside and deep, forcing safety Willie Wood over to help. Meredith eyes Hayes, but only as a decoy to hold Wood, then looks back to Clarke, who has run straight at safety Tom Brown, cut outside, then back inside, and straight upfield toward the goalpost (see diagram). The pattern, called a Z-out-and-post, twists Brown around and leaves him sprawled on the ground. Meredith lofts the pass to Clarke, twenty yards in the clear, and Clarke—like Meredith, one of the winless Cowboys of 1960—does the rest. Touchdown! The PAT makes it 34–27. The Cowboys have moved seventy-one yards in five plays—but most important, they have consumed only 1:01 on the clock. They are still alive.

Adderley returns Villanueva's short kickoff to the 28, and

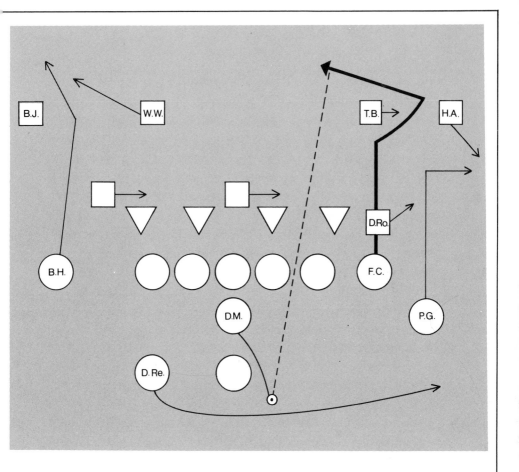

The intimidating speed of Bob Hayes (B.H.) sets up this play, a Z-out-and-post to the tight end, Frank Clarke (F.C.). As Don Meredith (D.M.) barks the signals, halfback Dan Reeves (D.Re.) goes in motion to the right, drawing the linebackers with him. Dave Robinson (D.Ro.), who had moved up into the line to play head-on against the tight end, now cannot impede Clarke's entry into the pass pattern. With Hayes drawing double coverage on the left from Bob Jeter (B.J.) and Willie Wood (W.W.), and flanker Pete Gent (P.G.) decoying Herb Adderley (H.A.) to the right, the middle of the field is open. Clarke jukes safety Tom Brown inside, outside, and down, and catches the pass in the clear. A sixty-eight-yard bomb on third and twenty!

the Packers have only to keep the ball for the remaining 3:50 to win their fourth championship in their last four tries. The hitch here is that in the second half, the Green Bay ground game has produced only twenty-five yards in twelve carries. So what does Starr do? He passes—to Fleming for eighteen! With Starr throwing the ball, a pass is as safe or safer than a run: this season, in 251 attempts, he was intercepted only three times, a record low.

But accurate as Starr may be, he cannot complete a pass while lying on his back. Dave Edwards blitzes from his right-linebacker spot and gets to Starr for an eight-yard loss. Bart's next pass is slapped down at the line by Townes. And on third and eighteen, at last he proves to be mortal, lifting a screen pass to Taylor which Lee Roy Jordan sniffs out for a loss of seven. The defensive unit leaves the field to an ovation, one arising from equal parts admiration and hope.

With the line of scrimmage the Green Bay 31, the ever-reliable Chandler shanks one—a wounded duck that travels only sixteen yards. Now the Cowboys are not merely alive—they are in business, with a first down at the Packer 47 and 2:19 to play.

Immediately, Meredith goes back to Clarke for twenty-one yards. The stadium is a madhouse. Perkins cracks the middle for four just before the two-minute warning. Next, Dandy Don throws deep for Clarke, who is being trailed by Robinson and Brown. To prevent the certain score, both defenders mug him at the 2. The pass flies by incomplete, but the refs have been watching: the obvious interference is called against Robinson, though it might as easily have been charged to Brown.

There's lots of time left—1:52, to be precise. Many in the stadium are thinking ahead to the Packers' next possession: Will they attempt to win the game in regulation, risking an interception, or will they run out the clock and take their chances in an overtime?

On first down and goal from the two, Reeves follows right tackle Neely, who has been dominating Willie Davis much of the game. But the play goes for only one yard, and this is why: For the last few plays, when pass-receiving ability was paramount, Norman had been replaced at tight end by Clarke. But now, this close to the goal line, the Cowboy bench sent Norman back into the game to play tight end, with Clarke, a fine blocker, to replace Hayes at the split end. A breakdown in communications resulted in *Clarke*'s leaving the game for Norman, keeping Hayes in to block ineffectively alongside Neely. Dallas showed its excitability and inexperience in this sequence, but they still have three shots from the 1-yard line.

On a great call, Meredith rolls right and throws in the end zone to Norman—who drops it. Even worse, the Cowboys' left tackle, Jim Boeke, broke from his three-point stance before the snap. The ball is moved back to the 6-yard line. This is a crippling blow, again a product of inexperience in pressure situations.

Second down again. Meredith tries a swing pass to Reeves— *who drops it*. The halfback had trouble seeing the ball, for his eyeball had been scratched on the previous play; yet he didn't tell the coaches or the quarterback of his injury, and hurt his team while doing his best to help it. Inexperience clouded his judgment.

On third down Meredith looks for Norman again, who has cut across the middle from left to right. Don rushes the pass, firing low and forcing Norman to break stride to make the catch; he gains four yards to the 2 before being brought down by Brown, but if the pass had been chest-high he would have carried it in for the score.

Fourth down and two, with forty-five seconds to play. This is it for Dallas. With the ball at the right hash mark, Meredith goes to the strongest of all goal-line plays, the rollout option. To cross up the defense, he will roll to the near sideline—which he hasn't done all year long. He will fake to Perkins off right tackle, hoping to freeze Robinson. Then Meredith will only have

Fourth and goal, with the championship in the balance. Dave Robin-son makes a great read and bursts through the line to nail Don Meredith—but not quite. "I thought I'd blown it," Robinson will say after the game. "I'm not supposed to let the passer get the ball off. I was sick to my stomach when he flipped it out there."

to worry about the cornerback, Adderley: If Adderley comes up to meet the run, Meredith will pass; if he hangs back, Meredith will run it in behind right guard Donohue. The key to the play will be the linebacker, Robinson—he must be held to his position by Perkins's fake, then blocked, at least momentarily, by the right end—who is *still* Bob Hayes rather than Clarke.

As the ball is snapped, however, Hayes's first move tells Robinson that the play is not coming off tackle; Perkins's fake is wasted. Robinson races to seal the outside, not daunted in the least by Hayes's brush block. As Meredith drifts out toward right end, there is Robinson waiting for him. His arms encircle Meredith, but pin only the left arm and right shoulder: Don is still able to flip the ball with a wrist motion toward Hayes, open in the end zone. The ball flutters softly to him—but safety Tom Brown picks it off! Brown, the victim of several long gainers to Clarke in this quarter, actually was assigned to cover Reeves on this play but lost him, and now emerges as the hero rather than the goat. The goat horns, if they must be worn, now remain on the heads of such Cowboys as Bob Hayes, Dan Reeves, Jim Boeke, Don Meredith—and Tom Landry.

Starr falls on the ball twice, and this wildest of all NFL championship games is over. Dallas and Green Bay combined for 785 yards, a record, in the kind of nonstop offensive display usually seen only in preseason games. How could these renowned defenses have been so bad? They weren't—it was just that the offenses were so good. To prove it, let me take you to Green Bay one year later, when these same teams will meet in a glorious rematch.

SCORING

PACKERS	14	7	7	6 — 34
COWBOYS	14	3	3	7 — 27

G.B.: Pitts, 17, pass from Starr (Chandler, kick).
G.B.: Grabowski, 18, fumble return (Chandler, kick).
Dal.: Reeves, 3, run (Villanueva, kick).
Dal.: Perkins, 23, run (Villanueva, kick).
G.B.: Dale, 51, pass from Starr (Chandler, kick).
Dal.: Villanueva, FG, 11.
Dal.: Villanueva, FG, 32.
G.B.: Dowler, 16, pass from Starr (Chandler, kick).
G.B.: McGee, 28, pass from Starr (kick blocked).
Dal.: Clarke, 68, pass from Meredith (Villanueva, kick).

TEAM STATISTICS

	Packers	Cowboys
First downs	19	23
Rushing yardage	102	187
Passing yardage	265	231
Punt return yardage	0	—9
Passes	19-28	15-31
Interceptions by	1	0
Punts	4-40	4-32
Fumbles lost	1	1
Yards penalized	23	29

INDIVIDUAL STATISTICS

RUSHES—G.B.: Pitts, 12 for 66 yards; Taylor, 10 for 37; Starr, 2 for —1. Dal.: Perkins, 17 for 108; Reeves, 17 for 47; Meredith, 4 for 22; Norman, 2 for 10.
PASSES—G.B.: Starr, 19 of 28 for 304 yards. Dal.: Meredith, 15 of 31 for 238.
RECEPTIONS—G.B.: Dale, 5 for 128 yards; Taylor, 5 for 23; Fleming, 3 for 50; Dowler, 3 for 49; McGee, 1 for 28; Pitts, 1 for 17; Long, 1 for 9. Dal.: Reeves, 4 for 77; Norman, 4 for 30; Clarke, 3 for 102; Gent, 3 for 28; Hayes, 1 for 1.

December 31, 1967

DALLAS
COWBOYS
VS.
GREEN BAY
PACKERS

Oh, how the Cowboys burned over that New Year's Day loss! The two yards they couldn't make in their final four downs cost them a crack at $15,000, the sum each Packer earned two weeks later by winning Super Bowl I against the champions of the renegade AFL. Driven by that memory, the Cowboys easily repeated as Eastern Conference champs to gain a shot at revenge this afternoon.

The question they had to ask themselves when they woke up in Green Bay this morning was whether they still wanted it. The thermometer read *sixteen degrees below zero,* making this the coldest New Year's Eve in Green Bay history. Postponing the match is impossible, largely because of television commitments; and playing indoors, as was done thirty-five years ago, would mean moving the game to another city, another impossibility. So the game will be played, today, at Lambeau Field, in arctic conditions never before encountered for an NFL championship contest. There are 50,861 Packer fans here for three hours of splendid misery.

As we near the kickoff time of 1:10, things have warmed up a bit—to a balmy thirteen below—but the northwest wind has not abated, blowing in at a biting fifteen miles per hour; the wind-chill factor comes to an awesome −38°F. The players will truly suffer: There are makeshift dugouts on each sideline with liquid-gas heaters, but these provide only momentary relief.

The footing is not bad—good enough, in fact, for cleats rather than sneakers—because Lambeau Field is equipped with underground electric heat, which has kept the turf from freezing during the week. Yet before the game begins, the heating system will break down, and the terrain will become harder and more slippery by the minute.

Does the cold give either team an edge? Dallas owner Clint Murchison, no doubt thinking back to Bart Starr's four touchdown passes against his club on New Year's Day, said: "It's too cold for the Green Bay passing game, and we'll win with our running." Unsaid but implied is the belief that Don Meredith will not be able to pass either, and that Green Bay's running game is inferior to that of the Cowboys. We shall see.

Dallas wins the toss, and will receive; the Packers choose to have the wind at their backs. Don Chandler, who this season lost his punting job to Donny Anderson, kicks off to rookie Sims Stokes; he returns the ball to the 33. The Cowboy offense takes the field, differing from last season's lineup only at center, where veteran Mike Connelly replaces the injured Dave Manders; and at flanker, where Lance Rentzel, acquired from the Vikings, has beaten out Pete Gent. The Green Bay defense has not changed at all, and once again was the league's best against the pass. If the Packers are able to win their third straight NFL championship game today, becoming the first team to do so, it will probably be the defense that does it.

On first down Meredith throws to Bob Hayes at the left sideline for ten yards. Dan Reeves follows Ralph Neely's block to the Cowboy 47. But that's as far as the Cowboys go on this series, as Meredith misfires to Rentzel and Reeves is racked up for no gain. Danny Villanueva punts into the wind to Willie Wood at the 16; he runs back only two yards.

The Packer offense also changed at center, where former backup Ken Bowman now starts in place of the traded Bill Curry. But more dramatically, the celebrated duo of Jim Taylor and Paul Hornung is gone from Green Bay—Hornung to an early retirement prompted by a string of discouraging injuries, Taylor to the expansion New Orleans Saints. Elijah Pitts, who filled in for Hornung in the New Year's Day game, was injured in midseason and will not play today. Nor will second-year fullback Jim Grabowski, who replaced Taylor and became the team's leading rusher before he too was forced from the lineup by injury. Starting at halfback this afternoon will be Donny Anderson, who has seen plenty of action since Pitts's injury; and at fullback, Chuck Mercein, a fringe player who was signed in desperation off the Washington Redskin taxi squad after serving earlier in the year with the New York Giants and the minor-league Westchester Bulls. The Dallas defense shows two changes: Mike Johnson and Jethro Pugh, both backups last year, for Warren Livingston at right cornerback and Jim Colvin at left tackle, respectively.

On first down, Starr hands to Anderson, who is led to a hole off left tackle by Mercein and Gale Gillingham; Anderson gains five yards, but fumbles. Fortunately Mercein is right there to pounce on it, or Dallas would have had a great chance to break out on top in a game that is not likely to provide much scoring. Anderson carries right for four, then over the middle for four

An All-American at Texas Tech and a first-round draft choice, Donny Anderson nonetheless warmed the Packer bench last year. On this frigid afternoon he'll be the team's workhorse.

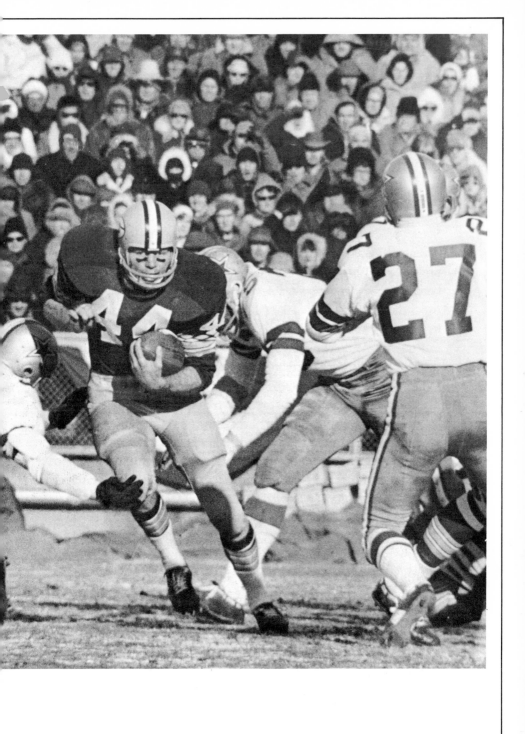

more and a first down. Now Starr drops back, his breath a trail of smoke; George Andrie and Bob Lilly follow that trail and drop Starr for a loss. The Cowboy hopes rest with the ability of their "Doomsday Defense" to harass Starr into hasty throws or losses.

On second and nineteen, Starr's pass for tight end Marv Fleming over the middle is broken up by Mike Gaechter . . . who is called for interference at the 31, an automatic first down. Starr comes back with a pass in the left flat to Anderson for seventeen. (Did you notice that the Green Bay offensive linemen are wearing gloves? The defensive linemen cannot wear them because they need to be able to grip firmly to throw blockers, or so they believe. Soon their hands will be so numb they won't be able to grip a thing.)

Runs by Anderson and Mercein bring up a third and five at the Dallas 47. Starr swings a pass out to Anderson, incomplete —but another critical error, a defensive holding call on Willie Townes, gives Green Bay a first down at the 42. Starr is so good at converting third downs that he hardly needs this kind of help. Two more runs by Anderson and Mercein produce a net of two yards, bringing up another third down. This time Starr needs no favors, hitting flanker Carroll Dale over the middle for seventeen.

An incompletion to Boyd Dowler is followed by another pass to Dale, this one good to the left sideline for fifteen. Starr is laying the ball up a little more softly than he might on a warmer day, but otherwise seems little troubled by the extreme cold. Anderson hits the middle for only a yard on first and goal from the 9. As Bart steps to the line for the next play, he notices that Dallas's backs are lined up to play man-for-man. This is not so unusual inside the 10-yard line: the backs can afford to play tighter on the receivers because they don't have to worry about being beaten thirty yards deep. But Starr instantly recalls that his split end Dowler has a six-inch height advantage on the man covering him, Mike Johnson: He calls an audible at the line to isolate

Dowler on Johnson, and hits him right in front of the goalpost. The sixteen-play drive has eaten up eighty-two yards in 8:50, aided enormously by those two timely infractions. Just as in the New Year's Day game, played in temperatures sixty-five degrees warmer, the Packers jump out to a 7-point lead with their opening possession.

Is this what Murchison had in mind when he said, "It's too cold for the Green Bay passing game"? He may have forgotten that today is not the first time Starr and Company have played in Green Bay in late December. Meredith and Associates, on the other hand, have never played in such conditions.

Chandler's kickoff is a low line drive. Lineman Larry Stephens gets his hands on the ball, deflecting it out of bounds at the 12, wretched field position. Fullback Don Perkins, coming off an outstanding year, carries for the first time in the game and gains five. Then Meredith hits Hayes at the right sideline for another five and a first down. This is the kind of pass which the sprinter has turned into long gainers countless times; but today the timing is off, for Meredith cannot "wing" the ball—throw it hard with a tight spiral—because he cannot wrap his frozen fingers around the football firmly enough. That tight spiral is absolutely necessary to cut through the gusting wind.

Three rushes by Perkins produce another first down, but then two incomplete passes and a futile run force Villanueva to punt. Wood calls for a fair catch at his 33. This time the Packers are unable to march down the field as they please; indeed, their three downs net only three yards, and Anderson punts weakly into the wind. Resuming possession where they last gave it up, at their 33, Dallas is in pretty good shape; for after Perkins's first-down run closes out the period, they can play fifteen minutes with the wind at their backs. Now is the time to put some points on the board.

Meredith's hands, however, are so frozen that his passes, even with the aid of the wind, soar out to his receivers like shot puts.

Boyd Dowler gets inside position on defensive back Mike Johnson, who is half a foot shorter than him. Bart Starr fires the pass high, and Dowler brings it down easily for the eight-yard score. The Packers have drawn first blood, just as they did in last year's title match.

His pass for Rentzel wobbles off the mark, and his toss to Reeves on third and ten is very nearly intercepted. Villanueva squibs a punt which rolls dead on the Green Bay 35.

The Packers come out with two new backs: journeyman fullback Ben Wilson, a former Ram, and Travis Williams, an exciting rookie whose four touchdowns on kickoff returns set an NFL record, but whose raw ability as a halfback needs harnessing. On first down Starr hands to Wilson, who barrels over the left side for thirteen. Now the give is to Williams, who also goes left, following Gale Gillingham and Bob Skoronski, for seven. On second and three from the Dallas 45, Williams tries the left side yet again, but this time the Cowboys stand their ground, holding the gain to two yards.

Third and one—the situation that has become known throughout the land as *belonging* to Bart Starr, so many times has he gone for broke in the air, taking advantage of a defense's tendency to overplay the run. The difference today, though, is that the gamble of throwing deep on third and one is heightened by the cold and the wind, which at the moment is blasting in Starr's face. *Nevertheless . . .* Starr fakes to Wilson, who plunges into the middle as the Dallas secondary hurries in, then heaves the ball as far as he can over the middle, where Boyd Dowler has beaten Mel Renfro. The pass appears to be way overthrown, but then the wind catches hold of the ball long enough for Dowler to run under it and make the fingertip catch in stride. Fourteen to nothing, same as the last time.

But where on New Year's Day the Cowboys had stormed back to a tie on their next two possessions, now they fail to move an inch on their first two plays after the kickoff, then cough up the ball on third down. Herb Adderley picks off Meredith's pass at the Dallas 47 and returns it fifteen yards. Green Bay has only to gain a few yards to move within field-goal range (remember, they are facing the wind).

With the game on the verge of becoming a runaway, the Cowboy defense stands tall. Linebacker Dave Edwards knocks down Starr's pass on second and ten, and George Andrie bursts through to nail Starr ten yards back on third down. We'll look back at this as a key play in the game.

Two punt exchanges follow, neither team having picked up a first down. With 4:20 left in the half, the Packers start a series at their 31. An illegal-procedure penalty on first down costs them five yards. Now Starr drops back, finds no one open, and retreats further as ends Willie Townes and George Andrie encircle the pocket. Just as Starr turns to scramble to the outside, Townes crunches him from behind. The ball pops free to Andrie, who takes it into the end zone! Dallas is back in the game, courtesy of an uncharacteristic Green Bay gift.

As the clock winds down on the first half, both offenses continue to sputter and stall in the deep freeze. Inside the two-minute mark, Villanueva punts from his 47. The ball tumbles end over end in the wind to Willie Wood, standing at the 17. He readies to make the catch, then thinks he ought to let it go, then decides to go for it after all. But it is too late. The plummeting brick (that's what it feels like when it hits his stinging, swollen hands) eludes Wood's grasp and is recovered by Dallas's Phil Clark.

Another great opportunity—yet still the Cowboys cannot muster an offense. On fourth and six with thirty-two seconds remaining in the half, Villanueva boots the 3-pointer.

Vince Lombardi is fuming. Dallas did not produce a single first down in the period, yet leaves the field trailing by only 14–10. (Not that the Packers' offense was any great shakes in the second quarter, either; they gained only two first downs, and those came on their opening drive.)

What are the coaches telling their men while they thaw themselves out in the locker rooms? Lombardi is suggesting that Starr abandon the longer pass plays because they take too much time to develop and place too much pressure on the offensive line. Tom Landry is suggesting to Meredith that he cut a hole in his jersey so that between plays he can keep his hands warm against his abdomen (Don completed four passes in the first half, for a total gain of only seventeen yards).

Villanueva dribbles his kickoff down to Lee Roy Caffey at the 37, not wishing to give Travis Williams a chance to break one all the way. Caffey returns to the 44, excellent field position, but the Packers continue to spin their wheels. Starr is dumped behind the line for the fifth time. Anderson punts to Rentzel, who signals for a fair catch at his 23 . . . and drops it. The ball skitters back toward the Dallas goal with both teams in pursuit. The alert Phil Clark again is first to fall on the ball, at the 11.

On first down, Meredith throws to Reeves for seven. Next, Perkins breaks through the line for eight, forcing safety Tom Brown to come up for the tackle. A first down! Now that the Cowboys have the hang of it, the yards begin to come in fistfuls. A pass to Frank Clarke is good for fourteen. Reeves hits the right side for eight and then twenty, and the left side for three, placing the ball on the Packer 29. Meredith finds Rentzel over the middle for another first down, the fourth of the drive, to the 18. But here the Packers show why they are great. Caffey spills Reeves for a loss of four, and a pass to Rentzel drops incomplete. On third and fourteen, Meredith is chased out of the pocket and scrambles for nine before he is clobbered by Caffey and stripped of the ball. Adderley recovers at the 13, to the muffled applause of gloved hands.

Green Bay gets out to its 27, then yet another sack forces yet another punt. Anderson's wind-tossed twenty-three-yarder sets the Cowboys up nicely, but they progress only far enough for Villanueva to attempt, and miss, a forty-seven-yard field goal.

With two minutes left in the period, Green Bay's offense tries again, with the now-familiar third-down sack culminating the series. Lombardi's halftime switch to shorter pass routes has not produced better results: The Packers have managed one first down this quarter, and Starr has been dropped three more times for a total of seven.

Opening the fourth quarter with a second and five at the 50, Meredith pitches out to Reeves, who sweeps left as both Packer backs on that side, Jeter and Wood, close in to play the run. This is a mistake. Reeves, a quarterback in his college days at South Carolina, pulls up short and flings the ball through the wind to Rentzel, all alone at the 20. He catches the ball in full stride and easily outruns Tom Brown to the end zone. Green Bay has been caught napping on one of its own favorite plays, the halfback option that Lombardi (and Landry) first popularized with the Giants. Only eight seconds into the quarter, Dallas finds itself on top 17–14. The margin is small, the time remaining is great . . . yet you can sense the mood of resignation in the stadium, a feeling that perhaps the dynasty wasn't meant to survive the departure of Hornung and Taylor, that the young Cowboys represent the future and the aging Packers belong to the past.

Neither team threatens in its next attempt, but Green Bay gets a break when, following Wood's punt reception at his 38, Dallas is assessed fifteen yards for a foolish face-mask violation. In the past, such a break could be relied upon to whet the Pack's appetite for a score. Do they still have the killer instinct?

On first down from the Dallas 47, Starr hits Dowler for thirteen yards to a burst of enthusiasm from the stands. But the rally is short-lived. The next three plays net only a yard, and on fourth down Chandler's field-goal try from the 40 is wide left.

An offside penalty gives Dallas a first down on its 31. Then, after two rushes by Reeves cancel each other for no gain, Meredith tosses to Clarke for ten. If Dallas can march down and score now, we can try to beat the rush to the parking lot. Perkins tries the left side, but Ron Kostelnik slips his block and wraps up the play at the line. No gain. Meredith looks to the right, then throws into the left flat for rookie Craig Baynham, in for Reeves—but the deception fails to deceive and Baynham is nailed for a loss of three. A third down toss over the middle to Rentzel is incomplete. The Green Bay defenders have done their job, and walk off to scattered hopeful cheers.

Following Wood's punt return, the offense comes on to the field with 4:50 to play. It is the twilight of the gods, and they must summon up every last bit of cunning and courage they possess. It is no secret that this game, if lost, will be Vince Lombardi's last as Green Bay's head coach, and that this year's Packer team does not really stack up against the four championship squads that have preceded it in this glorious decade. The Packers may not be back this way again for a while; it is this year's team that can seal the dynasty's place in history.

The Packers open up with a play-action swing pass to Anderson, good for six yards. With the underground electric heat having been out of commission the entire game, and the temperature dropping to eighteen below at this moment, the turf has become like concrete—there is no traction, which gives the edge to the offensive player because he can act, while the defender must react. With his blockers peeling out around right end and knocking linebacker Chuck Howley down, Mercein runs for seven and a first down at the Packer 45. Having established the threat of the swing pass, Starr now finds Dowler, who like Dale has been double-covered all afternoon, cutting over the middle for thirteen. Dowler is shaken up on the play, and is replaced by Max McGee.

Here the Packers court disaster. Anderson takes the pitch and sweeps right, looking to emulate Reeves and throw. It is an option play, but before Anderson can decide which option to exercise, the pass or the run, Townes swoops down from his end spot to throw him for a loss of nine. But Starr is not one to be fazed by a second and nineteen. He loops a little pass over the

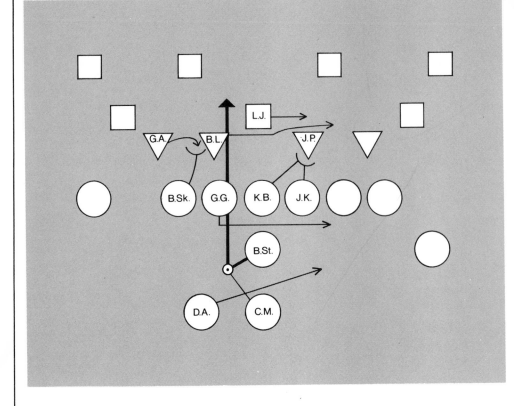

The Cowboys' Bob Lilly may be the best defensive tackle who ever played the game. Strong, quick, active, he is awfully tough to take out of a play. By making his quickness work against him, though, the "sucker" call illustrated above gets Lilly to take himself out of the play. As Bart Star (B.St.) whirls for the handoff, Donny Anderson (D.A.) crosses right, in front of Chuck Mercein (C.M.). Left guard Gale Gillingham (G.G.) pulls out of the line as if to block for a sweep by Anderson, luring with him both the middle linebacker, Lee Roy Jordan (L.J.), and, more importantly, Lilly (B.L.). Defensive end George Andrie (G.A.) loops behind Lilly to fill the vacated spot—but Bob Skoronski (B.Sk.) executes the critical block and seals him off. Ken Bowman (K.B.) and Jerry Kramer (J.K.) attend to Jethro Pugh (J.P.), and Mercein squirts through the gap for eight yards, down to the 3.

head of the onrushing front four to Anderson, who glides over the icy sod for twelve, eluding Edwards with a simple feint that, on a normal field, would have counted for nothing.

The two-minute warning is invoked. It is third down and seven from the 39, not really close enough for a field-goal try under these weather conditions. What to do? *Stay with what works until it stops working.* Starr comes back to Anderson again, for nine yards and the first down. The crowd's roar is constant now, seeming to echo in the frigid air.

With 1:35 left, Starr drops back, planning to throw to Dale or McGee—but he notices that in the left flat Mercein has floated out past Howley, who has slipped down. Bart flips to Chuck, who evades a tackler just past the line of scrimmage and lumbers down the sideline. He is knocked out of bounds at the 11, with 1:11 remaining.

This next play is a key one, for it is difficult to run the ball into the end zone from the 11 when just over a minute remains to be played. Yet with the tying field goal a virtual certainty, Starr is reluctant to risk a turnover by going to the air. The call is a "Give 65"—a "sucker" or "influence" play designed to take advantage of the great quickness of right tackle Bob Lilly, Dallas's perennial all-pro. Lilly's key to reading each play is supplied by left guard Gale Gillingham, lined up opposite him. Earlier in the game, when Gillingham pulled out to block on a run by Anderson to the right side of the line, Mercein was unable to cut down Lilly because the big tackle pursued the play on such a flat plane, parallel to the line. On this sucker play, Gillingham will pull out to the right as if to block for Anderson, hoping to draw Lilly with him; the handoff will then go to Mercein, who will try to slip through the spot vacated by Lilly. Essential to the success of this play (and to Mercein's survival) is the block which left tackle Bob Skoronski must execute on right end George Andrie, who will loop around to fill Lilly's spot (see diagram).

The play works beautifully—the hole opens up just as planned, and Mercein runs all the way down to the 3. After using the first of their three timeouts, the Packers gain a first down at the one on Anderson's plunge. Trying to conserve their remaining timeouts just in case, the Packers huddle quickly and come out to try a give to Anderson, again to the right between Forrest Gregg and Jerry Kramer. But this time Anderson has trouble with his footing, the hole doesn't open, and the play gets stacked up for no gain. Another timeout is called.

On second and one, with everyone standing, everyone yelling, Starr comes back with the same play. The hole seems to open wide enough for Anderson to squirt through, but he doesn't get to it in time. Slipping and sliding up to the line, Anderson arrives to find that the hole has closed; he is able to push the ball perhaps a foot closer to the goal. With 0:16 on the clock, the third and final timeout is consumed.

On the sidelines, Starr and the coaches discuss the alternatives. If they were to run and fail, the clock would not stop, and it is doubtful that the kicking team would be able to line up for the tying field goal in time. A pass would be the obvious call, for an incompletion would stop the clock, but it would provide the greatest chance of a turnover. The safest course, clearly, would be to kick the 3-pointer right now—but Lombardi won't go for that. As he will put it later: "We didn't want a tie. We had compassion for those spectators."

The call is a "31-Wedge" for Mercein, hitting a hole between right guard Jerry Kramer and center Ken Bowman. They will try to knock Jethro Pugh off the line by attacking him low, while right tackle Forrest Gregg keeps Willie Townes out of the play. The Packers take their positions. Starr shouts out the signals in little clouds of steam. The ball is snapped—but Mercein does not get it! While he carries out the fake toward the line, Kramer and Bowman drive Pugh back, and Starr dives for the end zone. He is in! With thirteen seconds to play, the Packers have done it!

All the chips are riding on this one. Bart Starr plows behind Jerry Kramer and Ken Bowman, both of whom are charging at Jethro Pugh (75). Chuck Mercein (30), who did not get the handoff on the "31-Wedge" called for him, is behind Starr, with the best seat in the house. This amazing gamble provides a fitting end to the Lombardi years, the glory years of Green Bay. It is the most famous touchdown in football history.

Fans cascade onto the field, hugging and pounding their heroes.

But the game is not over. The celebrants are herded to the sidelines, and Chandler kicks off into the end zone. Meredith passes incomplete to Rentzel, and then incomplete to Hayes, and now the game *is* over. The Cowboys trudge off the field heartbroken, having come so near—once again—and yet so far. But there will be other occasions for them. This time belongs to the Packers, at the end of their era.

SCORING

COWBOYS	0	10	0	7 — 17
PACKERS	7	7	0	7 — 21

G.B.: Dowler, 8, pass from Starr (Chandler, kick).
G.B.: Dowler, 46, pass from Starr (Chandler, kick).
Dal.: Andrie, 7, fumble return (Villanueva, kick).
Dal.: Villanueva, FG, 21.
Dal.: Rentzel, 50, pass from Reeves (Villanueva, kick).
G.B.: Starr, 1, run (Chandler, kick).

TEAM STATISTICS

	Cowboys	Packers
First downs	11	18
Rushing yardage	92	80
Passing yardage	100	115
Punt return yardage	0	19
Passes	11-26	14-24
Interceptions by	0	1
Punts	8-39	8-29
Fumbles lost	1	2
Yards penalized	58	10

INDIVIDUAL STATISTICS

RUSHES—Dal.: Perkins, 17 for 51 yards; Reeves, 13 for 42; Meredith, 1 for 9; Baynham, 1 for —2; Clarke, 1 for —8. G.B.: Anderson, 18 for 35; Mercein, 6 for 20; Williams, 4 for 13; Wilson, 3 for 11; Starr, 1 for 1.

PASSES—Dal.: Meredith, 10 of 25 for 59 yards; Reeves, 1 of 1 for 50. G.B.: Starr, 14 of 24 for 191.

RECEPTIONS—Dal.: Hayes, 3 for 16 yards; Reeves, 3 for 11; Rentzel, 2 for 61; Clarke, 2 for 24; Baynham, 1 for —3. G.B.: Dowler, 4 for 77; Anderson, 4 for 44; Dale, 3 for 44; Mercein, 2 for 22; Williams, 1 for 4.

January 12, 1969

NEW YORK JETS

VS.

BALTIMORE COLTS

The seers of Las Vegas predict that today's Super Bowl III will be every bit as dull as its two predecessors, crashing bores which ended in scores of 35–10 and 33–14. The betting line on today's interleague showdown pegs the New York Jets as 18-point underdogs to the Baltimore Colts. Indeed, most observers feel that the pro-football championship of the world was actually settled two weeks ago, when the Colts destroyed the Cleveland Browns 34–0 to capture the NFL title. That victory earned the Colts a holiday in Miami, which they intend to cap off with a few hours of light exercise worth $15,000 a man.

As the kickoff time approaches on this warm, cloudy afternoon in the Orange Bowl, let's review how these two teams came to be here. When Don Shula's Colts disposed of the Browns, they avenged the only defeat of their 13–1 season; by registering a shutout they ran their season's total to four, and made it six times that they had held their opponent without a touchdown. Relying on a rotating zone and a variety of blitzing tactics, the Colts' extraordinary defense permitted only 10 points per game.

And their offense wasn't too shabby either. Despite losing Johnny Unitas for virtually the entire year because of a bad elbow, the Colts racked up 29 points per game with surprise hero Earl Morrall at the helm. Morrall, a thirty-four-year-old veteran, had been a starter in only three of his previous twelve NFL campaigns. Shula had acquired him from the New York Giants during training camp only to back up Jim Ward, who was Unitas's backup. But when Ward was injured too, Morrall stepped into the lead role as if it had always been his. He threw for twenty-six touchdowns, ended the season as the NFL's highest-ranking quarterback, and was voted its Most Valuable Player.

Pitted against the conservative, defense-oriented Colts are the New York Jets, the mad bombers of a wide-open "basketball league" (haven't we heard that insult before?). The fifth outfit to challenge the NFL, and the fourth to take the name "American Football League," this AFL started play in 1960. At that time the New York entry was known as the Titans, and seemed as certain to go under as the S.S. *Titanic*. Bailed out by new ownership in 1963, the Titans were relaunched as the Jets, and they hired a new coach—Weeb Ewbank, recently canned by the Colts in favor of Shula. As he had done with the Colts, Ewbank embarked upon a five-year plan to construct a champion.

In 1965 the Jets took a large step in that direction by signing Joe Namath, a rookie quarterback from the University of Alabama, to a record-breaking $400,000 contract. This well-publicized act gave the AFL instant credibility, demonstrating

Joe Namath may not be the greatest quarterback of all time, or even his own time. But with his deep drop, quick release, slingshot arm, and penchant for throwing downtown, he is the most fun to watch.

that it had the means to lure top draft picks and even to engage in bidding wars for the NFL's established stars. Recognizing that this AFL would not just blow away as its three predecessors had done, the NFL made peace with it in 1966: The two leagues agreed to a common draft, an ultimate merger, and an annual Super Bowl.

The young quarterback whose signing brought all this about quickly became "Broadway Joe," the darling of New York football fans. In 1967 he passed for a record 4,007 yards; this year he, like Morrall, was his league's MVP. In the AFL championship game against the Oakland Raiders, he rallied his team from behind in the fourth period; he and Oakland's Daryle Lamonica combined to throw ninety-seven passes, to the amusement and scorn of the NFL. A few days before Super Sunday, Norm Van Brocklin, former quarterback of the Los Angeles Rams in their "basketball" days and now head coach of the Atlanta Falcons, was asked his opinion of Joe Namath, whose style had frequently been compared to his own. "I'll tell you what I think about Namath on Sunday night," he replied, "after he has played his first pro game."

In that remark you can see the Jets' motivation to win today —not only to glorify and enrich themselves, but also to vindicate their entire league. Earlier this week, the brash Namath spoke up for the AFL, saying that it offered at least five quarterbacks better than Morrall, and for his teammates, "guaranteeing" to the world that victory would be theirs despite what the odds-makers had to say. As you might imagine, the Colts' linemen can't wait to get their mitts on Broadway Joe.

The Jets have won the toss and will receive. Lou Michaels hammers the ball to Earl Christy two yards deep into the end zone; he runs it out to the 23. To the applause of the Orange Bowl's pro-AFL crowd, the high-powered Jet offense takes the field. Lining up in the backfield behind Namath are halfback

Emerson Boozer, one of the AFL's most dangerous runners until he ripped up a knee last year, and hard-driving fullback Matt Snell, who also is coming off knee surgery. New York is primarily a passing team, and these two are experts at picking off blitzers.

The first play is a simple handoff to Snell, who slants left behind the blocking of Boozer, tackle Winston Hill, and guard Bob Talamini. Snell gains three before linebacker Don Shinnick slips Boozer's block and makes the tackle. It is this simple play, with straight-ahead one-on-one blocking, that the Jets have made the key to their game plan on the ground. Snell will slant left without a predetermined hole to hit; rather, he will read his blocks and cut inside or outside to daylight. While viewing films of the Colts' previous games, the Jets found a weakness in the Colts' right side; and besides, the Jets' right side has a rookie, Randy Rasmussen, playing guard and a converted guard, the undersized Dave Herman, playing tackle opposite Bubba Smith. Bubba is six feet seven inches and 295 pounds, and in a game against Atlanta this season he actually lifted up a blocker and *threw* him at the ball-carrier, who was knocked down for a three-yard loss! You don't want to run Bubba's way too often.

On second down Namath calls the same simple slant, and Snell bursts through the line for nine. Safety Rick Volk comes up to make the tackle, but leaves the field hearing the whistle of freight trains. Snell is a bruiser. The Jets try the right side and the middle with far less success, though, and Curley Johnson punts the ball away.

Timmy Brown returns the kick to the Colt 27, and now we'll see how Shula plans to attack the Jets. Tom Matte and Jerry Hill are the backs—neither of them is what you would call a breakaway threat, but both are gritty runners who manage some-how to get the yards they must. Morrall's first play, however, is not a handoff but a nineteen-yard pass to John Mackey, the all-league tight end.

Having rocked New York back on its heels a bit, Shula now is ready to blast the Jets' line off the ball. He inserts Tom Mitchell into the lineup for blocking purposes, as a second tight end. Matte sweeps right for ten yards behind impressive interference. Hill sweeps left for seven more. The Colts are showing what they think of the AFL's best rushing defense. Next they hit inside for a first down at the New York 31. For Jet fans, this discouragingly methodical drive brightens as their all-league defensive end, Gerry Philbin, smothers Hill for a loss, and Morrall underthrows Jimmy Orr. But on third and thirteen Mitchell slips past safety Bill Baird and takes a pass all the way down to the 19. The Colts appear unstoppable.

But here they are stopped, as three pass plays produce not a yard. Coach Ewbank breathes a sigh of relief as the Colts' field-goal unit comes on: a 3–0 deficit is better than 7–0, he thinks . . . but Michaels blows the twenty-seven-yard kick!

Now Namath unveils the other half of the Jets' startlingly simple game plan: a short passing attack designed to strike underneath the tough Baltimore zone, executed quickly enough to blunt the blitz. On the first three plays of the series, Namath flips passes to Snell (incomplete), tight end Pete Lammons (two yards), and reserve halfback Bill Mathis (thirteen yards). Then, on first down from his 35, Namath heaves a pass with a purpose —a bomb to his flanker, Don Maynard, who has run a fly pattern straight up the right side.

Though Maynard has a step on safety Jerry Logan, the ball is way overthrown; still, this routine incompletion is a key play of the game. Maynard, whom you may remember as a return man for the Giants in 1958, overcame rejection by the NFL to become a star in the AFL. The home-run ball is his specialty, but this afternoon he suffers from a pulled hamstring which, while it permits him to run straight, prevents him from cutting. Seeing him outrun Logan up the sideline, Shula becomes convinced that the hamstring pull is not troubling Maynard: He decides to shade the Baltimore zone to Maynard's side of the field for the rest of the game. This is precisely what Namath wants; for Maynard's usefulness as a receiver today is severely limited, but as a decoy he can make things much easier for the other wide receiver, George Sauer. (In the 1958 sudden-death contest when Weeb Ewbank coached the Colts, Johnny Unitas's first-period bomb to Lenny Moore had the same effect, drawing coverage away from Raymond Berry's side of the field. Berry caught twelve passes that day.)

Namath now connects with Sauer for six, but then overthrows him on third down, forcing a punt. Despite excellent field position following Brown's twenty-one-yard return, Baltimore cannot move either. Its punter, David Lee, pins the Jets back on their 4-yard line with just under two minutes left in the quarter.

Standing over center on third down and one at the 13, Namath sees that the Colts are stacked up to stop the run with a seven-man line; daringly, he "audibles"—changes the play at the line of scrimmage—to a pass for Sauer. The quick toss is good for a first down, but at the 16 Sauer is hit by Lenny Lyles and fumbles. Reserve linebacker Ron Porter recovers the ball at the 12. Can the Colts be kept off the scoreboard now?

On the final play of the quarter—in which New York failed to cross midfield—Jerry Hill is dropped for a loss of one. Matte then takes a pitchout and sweeps left for seven. On third down Morrall spots Mitchell at the goal line, where he has a step on cornerback Randy Beverly. He fires the ball hard, but middle linebacker Al Atkinson tips it, deflecting the ball off course so that it bounces off Mitchell's shoulder pad straight up into the air. Beverly spins and races into the end zone to make the over-the-shoulder grab: interception!

The Jets are leading a very charmed life, but that cannot last for sixty minutes. They must begin to convince the Colts they are good as well as lucky.

Now Namath returns to the simple fullback slant that worked

so nicely at the start of the game. Snell dives off left tackle for one, then again for seven. Snell chugs around left end for six, and then again for twelve. The Colts' right flank, which is absorbing all this damage, is manned by three graybeards from the '58 sudden-death classic—end Ordell Braase, linebacker Don Shinnick, and cornerback Lenny Lyles.

As the Baltimore backs cheat in a few steps to aid in defending the run, Namath counters with an audible to Sauer, who gets behind Shinnick. Yet the pass flutters out weakly; Shinnick has a chance to intercept but, off-balance, manages merely to knock it down. Now it's second and ten to go, and Baltimore comes with its ferocious eight-man blitz—the four down-linemen, three linebackers, and the weak-side safety. But Namath smells it coming: he unloads the ball to Mathis for a gain of six.

On third and four the Colts repeat their all-out blitz, and again Namath beats it with his famous fast dropback and quick release; his pass to Sauer over the middle is good for fourteen, to the Baltimore 34. When Sauer saw safety Rick Volk creeping in for the blitz, he altered his pattern, breaking inside to Volk's vacated spot. Namath knew he would do so, and hit him (see diagram).

Namath is changing his calls at the line more than half the time now; he is plugged in to what Baltimore's aggressive defense is planning. He goes to Sauer again, who this time is covered tightly by Lyles—so tightly, in fact, that Lyles takes a gamble and goes for the interception. But the ball zings right through his arms and into Sauer's, for a gain of eleven.

A run by Boozer takes the ball to the 21. Namath, continuing to show contempt for the Baltimore pass rush, sends Snell out in the pass pattern rather than holding him in for blocking; the pass to him is good for another first down at the 9. Everyone in the stadium is stunned at the ease with which Namath is picking this great defense apart—no "basketball" plays, no long gainers, just old-fashioned, hard-nosed, so-called NFL football.

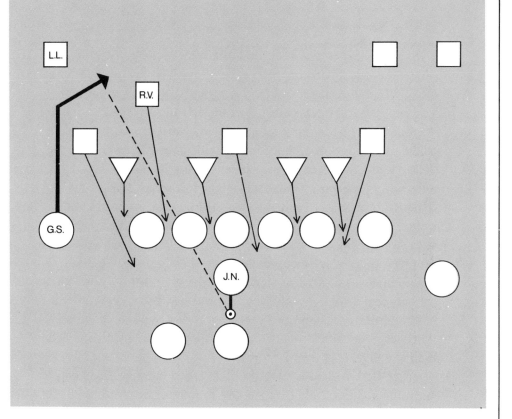

Baltimore comes after Joe Namath with an eight-man blitz. All three linebackers and the weak-side safety join the down linemen to over-whelm the Jet protection, but Namath (J.N.) and split end George Sauer (G.S.) have the answer. As soon as they notice safety Rick Volk (R.V.) creeping in, they read "blitz" and alter the pass play automatically. Sauer breaks off his prearranged route, cutting inside behind Volk, while Namath foregoes his customary deep drop and rifles the ball so quickly that the blitzers congregate at their target too late. The pass clicks for fourteen yards. However, veteran cornerback Lenny Lyles (L.L.) takes note of Sauer's response to Volk's key, and readies a countermeasure for the Colts' next eight-man blitz.

Snell makes five yards behind Hill and Boozer, breaking outside Shinnick's position before being tackled by middle linebacker Dennis Gaubatz. Then from the 4 Snell takes the handoff, cuts toward the hole between the left tackle and left guard, then dips outside and races for the corner of the end zone. Volk and Gaubatz follow in hot, but belated, pursuit. The Jets break on top! Jim Turner adds the point, making the score 7–0.

Preston Pearson returns the kickoff to the 28. On first down Morrall overthrows Willie Richardson, but comes right back with a flare pass to Matte, which he turns upfield for a juicy thirty-yard gain. Here the Jets get tough, though, with Johnny Sample—who played cornerback *for* the Colts in the sudden-death game a decade ago—cracking Mackey on third down and making him drop the pass. Sample wants badly to show the NFL, which drummed him out years ago, that he can still play. Michaels tries a field goal from the 46, but it is wide. The Jets get the ball back at their 20.

After Boozer goes over right guard for only a yard, Namath finds himself in an obvious passing situation. As he drops back against the Baltimore blitz, he looks for Sauer; cornerback Lyles now expects him to break over the middle into the vacated safety's spot, and moves over with him. What Lyles doesn't know is that Namath and Sauer had previously arranged that on the next Baltimore blitz Sauer would only fake inside, then run a fly up the sideline. And that's what Sauer does, outracing Lyles for a thirty-five-yard gain!

In Baltimore territory once more, Snell runs left for nine, then drives up the middle for three more. Maybe this game will be a rout after all—though not quite in the way folks had supposed. But here the Colt defense stiffens, hurrying Namath into two incompletions; then, on a third-down blitz, the Colts penetrate at last and force the weak-kneed Namath to "run" for a loss of two. Turner, who booted a record thirty-four field goals this year, comes on for a forty-one-yard attempt, but fails.

The Colts, burning with the humiliation of being the first NFL team to trail in the Super Bowl, return to the offense. Morrall finds Richardson for a gain of six. Next comes a handoff to Matte, who finds a hole off tackle, then is hit by safety Jim Hudson just as he gets past the line. But Matte tears himself from Hudson's grasp and suddenly finds he has clear sailing ahead. With the entire Jet defense behind him, Matte sprints upfield, seemingly headed for a touchdown. But speed is not one of Tom's many gifts—safety Bill Baird catches up with him at the 26 and knocks him out of bounds after a forty-eight-yard gain. The high-spirited Sample taunts Matte for failing to score. Two plays later, Sample adds injury to insult, intercepting a slant-in pass intended for Richardson at the 2. The crowd cheers in bewilderment—what kind of spell have the Jets cast on the Colts?

Unable to gain a first down on the ground, the Jets are forced to punt with less than a minute remaining in the half. Taking over on the New York 42, Morrall has ample time to position at least a field-goal attempt. On first down his wide receivers are covered, and a safety-valve pass to Hill yields only a yard. Now the solid, conservative NFL eleven resorts to a play that would make a sandlotter blush—a flea-flicker. Morrall hands to Matte, who sweeps right, stops, then tosses an overhand lateral back to Morrall. (Remember Harry Newman and Ken Strong?) Way downfield, all by his lonesome in the left corner of the end zone, stands Jimmy Orr, waving wildly for the ball—*but Morrall doesn't see him!* The way Earl turned to catch Matte's lateral left his back to Orr, and now all he can see to do with the ball is to catapult it to Jerry Hill, who is seemingly open at the 12, smack in the middle of the field. But as the pass descends toward Hill, Hudson races over, cuts in front of him, and picks it off. He is tackled at the 21 as time runs out on this shocking first half of play.

Sitting on the Baltimore bench having endured this debacle

Joe Namath hands off to Emerson Boozer while tackle Fred Miller views the scene with menace in his heart. Prior to today, patience was not one of the virtues associated with the New York offense. Yet here we are in the second half, and the Jets continue to play their cards close to the vest, with simple runs and short passes.

is Johnny Unitas, in uniform and partially recovered from his elbow injury. The line on him is that he can play if necessary, but cannot throw long. As the Colts trudge off to their locker room, Don Shula has already decided that Morrall, who has suffered three interceptions in the first half, will have one more series in which to redeem himself. If he stumbles again, in will come Johnny U.

On the first play from scrimmage in the second half Morrall, unaware of Shula's resolve, hands to Matte at the 25. Tom makes a few yards off right tackle, then is walloped by big Verlon Biggs, pursuing the play from the opposite end of the line. The ball squirts loose, and linebacker Ralph Baker falls on it at the 33. Nothing is going right for Baltimore today.

Boozer and Snell shred the line for two first downs, placing the ball at the 11. But then Boozer loses five on a botched sweep, and Namath is dropped nine yards further back by Bubba Smith. An incompletion to Lammons brings on Jim Turner, who this time splits the uprights from the 32, upping the count to 10–0.

Brown returns the kickoff to the 26, and the Colts come out led by Morrall. Since it wasn't Earl's fault that Matte fumbled, Shula is letting him have one more crack at the Jets. Perhaps now feeling the pressure to perform, Morrall opens with a bomb to Mackey, who is covered well by Hudson as the ball drifts beyond them. The Colts are only 10 points down with nearly twenty-five minutes to play; this kind of pass on first down betrays an unwarranted sense of panic.

On second down Morrall passes to Hill, who is tackled for no gain by linebacker Larry Grantham, one of three original Titans still with the club (the others are Maynard and Mathis). On third down, as the Jet linebackers take extremely deep drops to help out the secondary, Morrall once again can find no open receiver; he tries to run for the first down but doesn't come close. David Lee punts the ball to Bill Baird at the 32.

Namath keeps the Colt defense guessing. On his first series of the half he had relied on the run; now he returns to the air. Beating the blitz on second and nine, he finds Sauer over the middle for fourteen. After a misfire to Maynard, just to keep the defense worried about him, Joe connects with Lammons for eleven and another first down. From the Colt 38 he comes back to Maynard, overthrowing him on the fly pattern again, then flips to Snell coming out of the backfield for fourteen.

A draw play to Mathis is a clever call at this juncture, but it gains only a yard to the 23. Now Joe throws the bomb to Maynard still again, all the way to the back of the end zone. Don leaps to make a fingertip catch, but comes down beyond the end line.

The incompletion is not all that hurts the Jets on this play. Just as Namath released the ball, tackle Fred Miller broke through to clip his right hand, jamming the thumb that had been bothering Joe much of the year. The intense pain and numbness will prevent him from taking the third-down snap. Off the field he trots, replaced by Babe Parilli, a thirty-eight-year-old ancient who began his pro career with Green Bay back in 1952 and later shared quarterbacking duties with a rookie named Starr.

On third and nine, Parilli goes to Sauer over the middle, but underthrows him. Turner kicks the thirty-yard field goal to put the Jets on top 13–0.

How long will Namath be sidelined? With almost nineteen minutes to play, and Johnny Unitas coming in to give the Colts an inspirational lift, Namath's status is the central question of the game. While Namath attempts to throw on the sideline, Unitas calls his first play of the game: from the 20, Matte sweeps right for five. Now the master goes to the air—but the old magic is not there to be summoned up, not yet at least. Two incompletions force Baltimore to punt.

Namath is back! Taking over on his 37, he hands to Snell for a three-yard gain. Now we'll see whether he can grip the ball to pass—he goes to Sauer at the sideline, but the pass flies well over his head. The thumb hurts, he will reveal later, yet on third and seven he has little choice but to try again. This time he hits Sauer for eleven . . . and then again for a whopping gain down to the 10! The third period comes to a close, with the Jets having run off twenty-five plays to the Colts' nine.

Two rushes by Snell and one by Mathis fail to punch the ball in. With a fourth down at the 2, Ewbank recognizes the strategic value of 3 points at this stage in the game—you still force the Colts to score three times to win. Turner kicks the nine-yard field goal to lift the score to 16–0. The fans are growing accustomed to the formerly preposterous notion that the Jets may win—but where there's Unitas, there's hope.

Johnny U. sets up at his 27 knowing the Jets will play for him to pass on every down. His pass to Mackey is good for five. Matte sweeps right for seven. A pass to Richardson gains another five. Then Matte runs left for nineteen, and Hill runs right for twelve. Brilliantly, Unitas is crossing up the defense and producing large gains on the ground. The Colts huddle and come to the line quickly after each run, knowing that time is as much their enemy as the Jets. On first down from the New York 26, Unitas overthrows Richardson. Then Colt hopes, which had been slowly rising, are dashed again as Beverly cuts in front of Orr to intercept in the end zone.

Eleven minutes and six seconds remain in the game, so Baltimore is not dead yet—but they're sinking. Just as time is Baltimore's enemy, it is New York's ally; Namath will keep the ball on the ground and eat up as much of the clock as he can. From the 20, Boozer and Snell gain two yards apiece, setting up a third and six, a situation in which Namath might ordinarily be expected to throw. Joe will not throw another pass today. Refusing to risk an interception, he pitches back to Boozer who, to the dismay of the Colt bench, turns left end for the vital yardage.

Fullback Matt Snell, having the time of his life, runs by linebacker Mike Curtis on his way to a first down.

From the 31, even with the Colts overplaying for the run, Snell's standby, the fullback slant to the left, yields ten yards and another first down. In frustration, linebacker Mike Curtis tackles Snell with a little too much enthusiasm, and is penalized an additional fifteen yards to the Baltimore 44. The Colts must have the ball. Snell hits the middle for seven and Boozer follows with a gain of two over right tackle. On third and one, at last Baltimore comes up with the big defensive play, stopping Mathis for no gain. Turner misses the field goal from the 42, but this latest Jet drive, while it didn't put points on the board, consumed four and a half minutes.

The sun has set on Miami, and perhaps on the Colts as well, as Unitas trots out to try his hand one last time—if the Colts don't go all the way for the touchdown on this possession, the game is as good as over. He passes to Mackey, incomplete; to Richardson, incomplete; to Mackey again, incomplete. The Jets are ready to celebrate—but on fourth down and ten, Unitas reaches back through the years and comes up with a bit of nostalgia. He passes to Orr, complete at the 37, sustaining hope just as Baltimore's cause seemed its most hopeless.

Two more incompletions bring up a third and ten, which Unitas converts with an eleven-yarder to Mackey. He is fouled on the play for another fifteen yards. Passes of twenty-one yards to Richardson and eleven yards to Orr, plus another penalty, position the ball on the Jet 2. The crowd is buzzing now, sensing that Unitas, the best the sport has ever seen in the closing minutes of a game, may be about to produce his miracle of miracles.

Matte tries to get into the end zone behind left guard Glen Ressler, but is halted for no gain. Nonetheless, the ball is moved up to the 1 as the Jets are ruled offside. It is still first and goal. Unitas tries a sneak, but is stopped by Biggs. Matte tries to follow right guard Dan Sullivan, but fails. On third down, Hill finally bursts across the line behind the block of left tackle Bob Vogel. However, by forcing the Colts to run four times from the 2, the

Jets have deprived them of priceless seconds. Only 3:19 is left, and after Michaels's PAT the Colts trail by nine, 16–7.

You know that an onside kick is coming, just as everyone in the Orange Bowl does. But forewarned is not forearmed, in this case, as Michaels's dribbler bounces off Sauer (who had been placed at the N.Y. 40 for his great hands) and into the mitts of Baltimore's Tom Mitchell! The Colts run onto the field, knowing they must strike quickly and then recover *another* onside kick, a feat bordering on the impossible. But here comes Unitas—to Richardson for six; to Orr for fourteen; to Richardson for five. In an instant, the Colts have moved to the Jet 19. The Orange Bowl is buzzing now.

Second and five. A pass to Richardson—tipped away by Sample. Third and five. A pass to Orr—short. It is fourth and five. The game will be decided now. The crucial pass loops toward Jimmy Orr in the end zone—but is slapped away by Grantham!

It's over. The greatest upset in the history of professional football is over, no matter that two minutes and twenty-one seconds remain to be played. Snell will carry the ball six consecutive times until the Jets are forced to punt, and with eight seconds remaining Unitas will throw two more desperation passes, but this is mere ritual. The Jets, and the AFL, have won.

The year 1969 will see further improbabilities—man will walk on the moon and the New York Mets will win the World Series. But the Jets winning the Super Bowl? No, that was not improbable; it was impossible—to everyone but Joe Namath and the Jets.

SCORING

JETS	0	7	6	3 — 16
COLTS	0	0	0	7 — 7

N.Y.: Snell, 4, run (Turner, kick).
N.Y.: Turner, FG, 32.
N.Y.: Turner, FG, 30.
N.Y.: Turner, FG, 9.
Bal.: Hill, 1, run (Michaels, kick).

TEAM STATISTICS

	Jets	Colts
First downs	21	18
Rushing yardage	142	143
Passing yardage	195	181
Punt return yardage	0	34
Passes	17-29	17-41
Interceptions by	4	0
Punts	4-39	3-44
Fumbles lost	1	1
Yards penalized	28	23

INDIVIDUAL STATISTICS

RUSHES—N.Y.: Snell, 30 for 121 yards; Boozer, 10 for 19; Mathis, 3 for 2. Bal.: Matte, 11 for 116; Hill, 9 for 29; Morrall, 2 for —2; Unitas, 1 for 0.

PASSES—N.Y.: Namath, 17 of 28 for 206 yards; Parilli, 0 of 1. Bal.: Morrall, 6 of 17 for 71; Unitas, 11 of 24 for 110.

RECEPTIONS—N.Y.: Sauer, 8 for 133 yards; Snell, 4 for 40; Mathis, 3 for 20; Lammons, 2 for 13. Bal.: Richardson, 6 for 58; Orr, 3 for 42; Mackey, 3 for 35; Matte, 2 for 30; Hill, 2 for 1; Mitchell, 1 for 15.

November 8, 1970

DETROIT
LIONS

VS.

NEW ORLEANS
SAINTS

All of the great games we have seen thus far have been played in championship settings, as befits them. But greatness can sometimes emerge from the least promising of surroundings, as we will see this afternoon.

It is 1970, and the NFL has celebrated its fiftieth birthday by absorbing the AFL into a newly aligned six-division league, split into two conferences: the AFC and the NFC. For the New Orleans Saints, this peaceful resolution of the war between the leagues means merely that rather than being the worst of the NFL's sixteen teams, it can now lay claim to being the worst of its twenty-six. After a loss to the Rams last Sunday brought the Saints' mark to 1–5–1, coach Tom Fears, who had headed the club since its inception in 1967, was dismissed. In his place management hired an unheralded minor-league coach, J. D. Roberts. This afternoon he will throw his Saints to the Lions of Detroit, who are 5–2 and playoff-bound.

The Lions are a solid club—good passers in Bill Munson and Greg Landry, hard runners in Mel Farr and Altie Taylor, the league's best defense against the rush, and a secondary and linebacking crew that will lead the league in interceptions. The Lions have, in short, everything the Saints lack—except perhaps the motivation to play above their heads for a new coach. At least, that's the hope of the 66,910 people who have packed Tulane Staduim.

Kicking off for New Orleans is Tom Dempsey, who is a story by himself. Born with only half of a right foot (his kicking foot) and a shortened right arm that ends in only two fingers, the 265-pound Dempsey overcame these handicaps. He played in the line and placekicked in high school, in junior college, and then in the Atlantic Coast Football League. As a semipro Dempsey kicked barefooted, with a strip of tape across his toe-less foot. But when he earned a professional trial with the San Diego Chargers in 1968 (he didn't make the club), he had to wear a specially constructed box-type shoe, for NFL regulations at that time prohibited barefoot booters. Last year he landed with the Saints and did a fine job, kicking twenty-two field goals; one of these traveled fifty-five yards, only a yard short of the NFL record.

Dempsey's kickoff sails into the arms of Bobby Williams at the 26. The Lions come out on offense led by Bill Munson at quarterback. Coach Joe Schmidt has split the signal calling between Munson and the younger Greg Landry for two years now, to the dissatisfaction of both men; but the Lions move the ball equally well with either at the helm. Behind Munson are running backs Mel Farr and Altie Taylor, both swifties. Neither

Tom Dempsey made it to the NFL despite his birth defects. Though he modeled his kicking style after Lou Groza, he may also have drawn inspiration from Ben Agajanian, another toeless placekicker.

is large enough to fit the classic mold of a fullback, however, and this represents one of Detroit's weaknesses, especially in short-yardage situations. Munson's wide receivers are Earl Mc-Cullouch and Larry Walton, both fleet and sure-handed, and the tight end is Charley Sanders, a rising young star who will supplant Baltimore's John Mackey as the best at his position. The offensive line is experienced and effective, particularly at firing out for the run.

On the first play from scrimmage, Farr cracks left tackle for three. Then Munson hits Sanders crossing over the middle for ten yards and a first down at the 39. Now Taylor, too, tries his luck off left tackle, but manages only a yard. Munson comes right back over the middle for another completion, this time to Walton for seven. Third and two, the first important play of the game. Stopping the Lions here would do wonders for the Saints' morale; and conversely, allowing Detroit to march down the field for an opening score might lay the groundwork for a rout.

The Saints stack up for the run, with the linebackers poised to fill the gaps. Farr takes the handoff and leaps over the right side, but New Orleans's left end Richard Neal and middle line-backer Dick Absher stand tall, throwing Farr back shy of the first down. The success-starved crowd greets this development as fervently as if it were a goal-line stand in the closing moments of the Super Bowl. The fans will be a twelfth man on the field for the Saints today; whether twelve will be enough remains to be seen.

Herman Weaver punts the ball to the 6-yard line, where Al Dodd fields it and returns to the 20. Dodd stays in the game at wide receiver, which may be the Saints' best-stocked position what with Danny Abramowicz, last year's league-leading pass-catcher, on the opposite end of the line. The tight end, Ray Poage, is a solid receiver but does not see too many balls thrown his way.

The running backs are Tom Barrington and Jim Otis. Unlike

Detroit, which can be said to have no true fullback, the Saints field two of them, which presents a different kind of problem—how to run wide or far. At quarterback is the veteran Bill Kilmer, who came to New Orleans in the expansion draft after several injury-plagued years with San Francisco. Billy doesn't throw the prettiest passes you've ever seen, but he has the force of will that makes for a good field general.

New Orleans's first play is a handoff to Barrington, who hits the right side for eight. The next play returns to the scene of attack, with Barrington gaining three yards and the first down. The Saints' game plan calls for them to go straight at Alex Karras, a great tackle who, at the age of thirty-four, is past his prime, and Jim Mitchell, a rookie end who, at the age of twenty-one, has much to learn.

After overthrowing Poage on first down, Kilmer unloads a bomb to Dodd, who is in the clear up the left sideline. The pass connects for forty-one yards—but wait . . . there's a yellow flag just behind the line of scrimmage. The call is holding, a fifteen-yard penalty which winds up costing the Saints fifty-nine yards. The crowd groans, having seen this sort of thing all too often before; the Saints' offensive line, a patchwork quilt of aging castoffs and overmatched youngsters, often must resort to holding if it is to keep Kilmer in one piece.

On their next two downs the Saints recover some of the yardage they lost, but not enough to maintain possession. Julian Fagan, the rookie punter, gets away a boomer of forty-nine yards, driving Detroit's Nick Eddy back to the 26. Eddy retraces his steps as far as the 32, where he is hit and fumbles. Hugo Hollas recovers for New Orleans.

Jim Otis gains three on first down; this is followed by Barrington's gain of five. Both runs are again directed at Karras and Mitchell. Needing two yards to keep the drive going, Kilmer rolls right and flips to Poage at the right sideline for three. But this is as far as the Saints will march—Kilmer's next three passes fail to move the ball, so in comes Dempsey to try his luck from the 29.

Tom knows he had better start getting lucky today, or he may soon find himself on the outside looking in. Through the first half of the season he has connected on only five of fifteen field-goal attempts, a percentage that does not lead to career longevity. But this time Tom's straight-on kick, modeled after the style of Lou Groza, is true. New Orleans leads 3–0.

After Dempsey's kickoff bounds through the end zone, Detroit moves briskly from its 20 to midfield. Taylor sweeps left end for twelve and, following a pass to McCullouch, sweeps the opposite end for seven more. But on third and three, when a power play might be the ticket to a first down, Munson sends Taylor on another sweep right—and Absher slides over from the middle to cut him down.

Weaver's short punt takes a backward bounce, enabling the Saints to set up at their 32. Kilmer sticks with what has been working, sending Barrington and then Otis barreling through Karras and Mitchell for a first down. The ease with which Del Williams and Errol Linden are knocking these defensive linemen aside is astonishing—Detroit will have to make some adjustment.

The first quarter ends with the Saints at midfield, confronting a third and five. When play resumes, Abramowicz drives cornerback Lem Barney back, then cuts to the right sideline, where Kilmer's six-yard pass awaits him—first down! The pace of the game is slow, but New Orleans is doing what it has to do: control the ball, which keeps its shaky defense off the field and holds the score low enough for its feeble offense to stand a chance of outpointing Detroit.

Otis powers over the right side for four yards and then five, but on the latter play center Jerry Sturm brings the drive to a grinding halt: He is called for holding, a flagrant blunder on a running play. After Fagan punts fifty-two yards into the end zone, Detroit starts from its 20. Farr sweeps right for six, then Taylor takes the same route for eleven. Now Munson tries to vary his attack, going long to McCullouch, but overthrows him. A clumsily executed screen pass produces a third and ten, which Munson converts with a bullet over the middle to Walton for sixteen. Runs by Taylor and Farr bring up another third-down situation at the Saints' 44, which Munson converts again, this time with a pass to Sanders for thirteen. Nothing does more for a quarterback's, and a team's, confidence than a couple of third-down conversions. On third and nine from the Saint 30, Munson again connects with Sanders, this time over the middle, all the way to the 13-yard line.

The Lions are chewing up the Saints now. On first down Taylor sweeps left end for three. Then Munson drops back, but slips the ball to Farr on a draw play. Tackles Mike Tilleman and Dave Rowe take the bait, charging past the offensive linemen's token resistance, and Farr bolts up the middle for the score. Errol Mann adds the point, and every Saint fan thinks, "Here we go again."

Rookie Ken Burrough, who in later years will become a star with the Houston Oilers, returns Mann's kickoff to the 31. On third down from the 37, Kilmer hits Abramowicz for ten and the more trusting fans take heart again—but then a twelve-yard rush by Otis is, incredibly, called back on yet another offensive-holding call, this time on guard Jake Kupp. One step forward, two steps back. Fagan punts to the 15, where Walton makes a fair catch.

On first down Munson drops back to pass, sensing that the Saints are ripe for the taking. Feeling some pressure from the rush, he scrambles right and lofts a pass to Sanders, complete for twenty-nine yards. The rumblings of discontent in the stadium grow louder. But then the gritty Saints drop Farr for a loss of two and, on third and eight, come up with a big play—Joe Scarpati intercepts a pass intended for McCullouch.

The Saints go back on the "attack" at their 36 with 1:33 left in this admittedly humdrum first half of play. On first down Kilmer finds Poage over the middle for twelve. Otis dives left for seven to the Lion 45. But while Kilmer is dumping a flare pass to Otis, one of the Saints' linemen has mysteriously drifted downfield and been spotted by an official—*another fifteen-yard penalty.* On second and long Kilmer underthrows Burrough, then on third and long he returns to Burrough—who is assessed *another fifteen yards* for offensive pass interference. This takes the patience of a saint, and not of the New Orleans variety.

Fagan punts to Eddy at the 31. The former Notre Dame star scoots back to the 39, where he fumbles again! Recovering the football for the Saints is Elijah Pitts, the former Green Bay back playing out the string down south.

So this is a great game, you say? Not yet, I grant you, but remember, the first half of the 1958 sudden-death classic wasn't much better.

With thirty-three seconds on the clock, Kilmer looks to throw. His receivers downfield are covered, so he tries to slip a pass to Otis at the right sideline—incomplete. Next he sends the speedy Dodd on a fly pattern, but overthrows him. On third and ten, however, Kilmer connects: Abramowicz finds the seam in the zone twenty yards over the middle. The Saints call time with fifteen seconds left.

Huddling on the sideline with Coach Roberts and assistant coach Don Heinrich, Kilmer agrees to try a pass into the end zone; if that fails, there'll still be time for a field goal-attempt. From the 19, Kilmer arches one toward Ray Poage at the goal line, but safety Wayne Rasmussen tips it away. Dempsey comes on and, with nine seconds to play, boots the twenty-seven-yard field goal to make the score 7–6. The Saints haven't looked particularly good on offense or on defense, yet they leave the field very much in contention against a superior foe. If only they could stop taking those momentum-killing penalties. . . .

But they can't. On their second play from scrimmage in the

second half, Jerry Sturm is again called for holding on, of all things, a draw play. Following Fagan's first weak punt of the day, a thirty-one-yarder, Detroit takes over at the Saint 48.

Seeking to capitalize on this fine field position, Munson goes to the air immediately, looping a pass to Sanders down the left side. But linebacker Jackie Burkett, a veteran cast aside by the Colts, crosses in front of Sanders to intercept, and returns sixteen yards to the Lion 44.

The Saints' first two plays are handoffs to Otis, off left tackle for six and then three. On third down and one, Kilmer calls the play to go the other way. As so often happens when a defense overplays for the short-yardage dive, a big gainer results if the back can penetrate the line and stay on his feet. Hoping merely to gain the necessary yard, Barrington bursts through the seven-man line and rumbles downfield for nineteen.

But the Lion defense once again assumes control, bringing Dempsey in to attempt a twenty-four-yarder that will give New Orleans the lead. The snap and the hold are good, but Dempsey doesn't get under the ball: he hits a line drive which the charging Jim Yarbrough swats aside. The bouncing ball is picked up by Dick LeBeau, who scampers thirty-seven yards to the Saint 45.

This time the Lions will not be denied. Farr circles left end for sixteen yards, and Taylor follows suit with six. A pass to McCullouch connects for fifteen yards, down to the 8. Here right end Dave Long makes a big play, dumping Taylor for a loss of one, but this interruption of Detroit's drive is only momentary. Chased out of the pocket on a second-down pass attempt, Munson manages to scramble to the 2. On third down he drops back once more, and locates Sanders crossing from right to left in the end zone—touchdown.

After adding on the point, Mann jolts the crowd—and the Saints—with a surprise onside kick. The ball bounces erratically between, off, and past several of the Saints, and is covered by Detroit's Bobby Williams. Coach Schmidt, sensing that the Saints are on the ropes and dazed after the blocked kick and ensuing touchdown, is trying to put them down for the count with this haymaker. But the Lions' game-long bugaboo, the turnover, keeps the Saints in the thick of things: On first down Munson, looking to go long, is swallowed up by Mike Tilleman and fumbles; the Saints' other tackle, Dave Rowe, recovers at the Lion 47.

Kilmer moves his club down to the 7-yard line with two passes to Abramowicz and one to Otis, but then turns conservative. Three rushes off right tackle move the ball to the 1, and a decision must be made: should Roberts play to the crowd's sympathies and go for 6, or pull in his horns and take the automatic 3? What would you do in this spot, with under a minute left in the third quarter and your club trailing 14–6?

Roberts doesn't want to have his men come this far and walk away empty-handed; so Dempsey boots the eight-yarder and the Saints hang tough at 14–9. Each of their three scores has been positioned by a Detroit turnover (and so was the missed field-goal attempt).

Williams returns Dempsey's kickoff to the 20 as the gun sounds, ending the third quarter of play. An exchange of punts follows, then Detroit's next possession is terminated by Munson's third interception of the day and the second collected by Jackie Burkett. The linebacker once again outduels the formidable Charlie Sanders for the ball, and sets his club up at the Detroit 34 with 10:19 to play. Sensing that the once unlikely prospect of victory is suddenly within reach, the fans spur their tattered heroes on.

Otis lumbers over left tackle for six, and then over right tackle for seven more. Kilmer flips a pass to Barrington in the right flat, but Mitchell makes a fine play to haul him down for no gain. On second down from the 21, Kilmer goes to Abramowicz, who dives to smother the low throw near the left sideline; the official, however, rules the catch a trap. Third and ten, and Kilmer comes back to his favorite receiver, this time connecting

One in a long line of Ohio State fullbacks to reach the NFL, Jim Otis is a powerful 225-pounder, but no breakaway threat. He needs to operate behind a quality offensive line, which the 1970 New Orleans Saints cannot offer. His career will be stuck in low gear until he is dealt to the St. Louis Cardinals. Five years from now, running behind such all-pros as Dan Dierdorf, Conrad Dobler, Tom Banks, and Bob Young, Otis will be the NFC's leading rusher.

for thirteen vital yards. New Orleans has a first and goal from the 8.

The Saints were down here not so long ago, played it close to the vest, and had to settle for 3. But Kilmer has not learned from history, and so repeats it. Otis gains only two yards on first down, then one more on second down. But . . . oh, no—left guard Jake Kupp, trying to clear a path for Otis, was caught holding tackle Jerry Rush. The Saints are pushed back to the 20. The only consolation in this catastrophic penalty is that Dempsey might well have had to kick a field goal from inside the 5, and now he'll find it nearly as easy to kick one from inside the 30.

On second and goal, Kilmer throws for Al Dodd in the end zone, incomplete. But now Detroit, which has not been called for a penalty all afternoon, commits a devastating one: pass interference, by Lem Barney against Dodd at the 4! The fans go wild —with the automatic first down, their team has been given another life, another chance to score the go-ahead touchdown. And the Saints waste no time scoring it: Kilmer calls his most reliable running play, Barrington over the right side between Del Williams and Erroll Linden, and New Orleans takes the lead, 16–14.

The fired-up Saints' special team races downfield under Dempsey's kickoff, and Doug Wyatt nails Jerry Williams at the 14. The Lions come out with a new captain at the helm replacing Munson—Greg Landry, the second-year man who already has made a reputation for himself as one of the best running quarterbacks since Otto Graham. Wisely, he makes his first call a ground play, on which Farr gains six around left end. More than six and a half minutes remain in the game, so there's no need to panic and fill the air with footballs; and besides, a few handoffs will loosen up the bench-ridden Landry. Taylor slips off left guard for three on the next play, and then Farr plunges for the first down.

Now, at the 25, Landry drops back to try his first pass, a medium-range pass to Walton; it misses the mark by a wide margin. On second down he throws over the middle to Mc-Cullouch, who makes the catch at the 40—but only after the ball had been tipped by another Detroit player. In the years to come, this kind of volleyball action will present no problem, but in 1970 it is illegal. One member of an offensive team may not, intentionally or otherwise, bat a pass to another; such a play is ruled a simple incompletion. Correctly, the officials bring the ball back to the 25—but neglect to change the down marker! *And no one on the field seems to notice.*

Following his two missed passes, Landry scurries back under pressure and tries to swing the ball out to Farr, but underthrows him. You and I know that this ought to bring up a fourth down and ten and a certain punt, but down there on the turf, the teams are lining up head to head for what they believe to be a third-down play. The stadium is buzzing with the queasy feeling that something is wrong; but Landry fades, looks to the left sideline, and fires to McCullouch for ten yards and a highly unorthodox first down.

After overthrowing McCullouch on his next pass, Landry hits Walton over the middle for nine. On third and one he keeps the ball himself for four yards and another first down at the Detroit 48. There's still plenty of time to get downfield, so Landry gives to Taylor on the sweep right that has been so effective. But linebackers Mike Morgan and Absher do a good job of stringing the play out to the sideline, and cornerback Wyatt comes up quickly to knock Taylor out of bounds after a gain of three. Altie takes exception to the way he is pushed out, however, and flails at Wyatt. This show of temper costs his team fifteen yards.

Naturally, the crowd is delighted to see the ball come back to Detroit's 36 for a second down and twenty-two. But the delight is short-lived indeed, for the very next play brings a call of pass interference on Hugo Hollas, an extra defensive back who hammered Larry Walton at the Detroit 49.

Bolstered by this break, Landry then finds Sanders on the left side for seventeen as the two-minute warning is delivered. The ball is at the 34, already within Errol Mann's range, but one or two more first downs would not only improve Mann's chances, but also consume time New Orleans might use in its final attempt to rally. So Detroit can afford to keep the ball on the ground, and does, as Farr cracks left for four yards. Then, in a deft move from the 30, Landry calls his own number, sweeping right end on a keeper for thirteen important yards.

The air is tense; everyone in the seats and on the field is ready to concede Detroit the go-ahead field goal, and concentrates instead on the clock. The Lions will run it down as far as they can. With 1:11 left, Farr gets a yard off right guard. The Saints cannot call timeouts because they may need them on the offense—they can only concentrate on producing a fumble, or blocking the forthcoming kick.

Forty-two seconds to go. Landry takes the ball straight up the middle for seven. The clock continues to run. On third and two at the 9, with seventeen seconds remaining, Farr runs left and is hauled down for a loss by Absher—ordinarily a big play, but in this situation not terribly important. At 0:14, the Lions call timeout to get their kicking unit on the field without slipup. And the kick by Mann is good! The Lions, evident victors by a score of 17–16, have consumed six minutes and thirty-one seconds, driving eighty-six yards in seventeen plays—an impressive demonstration of how cream will rise to the top.

The Saints have given a good accounting of themselves for their new coach; and the fans, though certainly disappointed, have to give their Saints credit. After all, Detroit had to have an "extra" down to win!

As the fans start to file out of the stadium, Mann kicks off to the 14-yard line. Dodd collects the ball and zips toward the sideline, stepping out at the 28 with 0:08 showing on the clock. This going-through-the-motions part of the game is aggravating to the fans and disheartening to the players on the losing side, but football is a sixty-minute game.

There's time for at least one more play. Kilmer takes a shallow drop, then throws down the left sideline to Dodd, who is being given a wide berth by cornerback Dick LeBeau; LeBeau's only concern is to keep the Saints out of field-goal range. Dodd catches the ball and steps out at his own 45 with two seconds to play, so LeBeau has done his job.

The Saints call timeout to discuss what they should do with their final play. At the sideline, J. D. Roberts asks his assistant, Don Heinrich, "What's next, Don?"

"We've got to go for the field goal," Heinrich says. It seems preposterous to talk of a field goal of sixty-two or more yards when the NFL record of fifty-six has stood since 1953; yet is it more preposterous than trying to dream up a play that will go for a fifty-five-yard touchdown with two seconds to play? Heinrich knows that Dempsey, erratic as he has been this season, can kick the ball as far as anybody. His handicap—the kicking foot without toes or instep—is actually an asset when it comes to kicking from far out, because Dempsey, unlike all other kickers, does not have to use part of his muscle-power to lock his ankle and hold his instep firm. But there's not so much science behind Heinrich's spontaneous decision; his choice is based on necessity and desperation.

The kicking unit comes on the field. Holder Joe Scarpati confers with Dempsey; they agree to place the ball one yard further back than the customary seven yards behind scrimmage. They realize that if the kick is to have any chance, it cannot spend its energy in excessive height; remembering how Dempsey's line-drive kick was smothered in the third period, they choose to set up eight yards back to foil a potential block.

So, as the Lions half-heartedly line up—one of them is even laughing—Scarpati kneels at the New Orleans 37. Dempsey stands a step and a half back, concentrating not on the sixty-three yard distance, but on kicking the ball straight, and just high enough.

The snap is good, the placement correct, and Dempsey puts everything he has into the kick. The ball rockets off his foot as

Everyone in Tulane Stadium is dubious about this final play of the game; the Detroit Lions' personnel on the sideline seems particularly skeptical. From Joe Scarpati's hold, Tom Dempsey attempts a field goal from 63 yards out. In NFL history, no one has ever succeeded from this distance. No one has even dared to try.

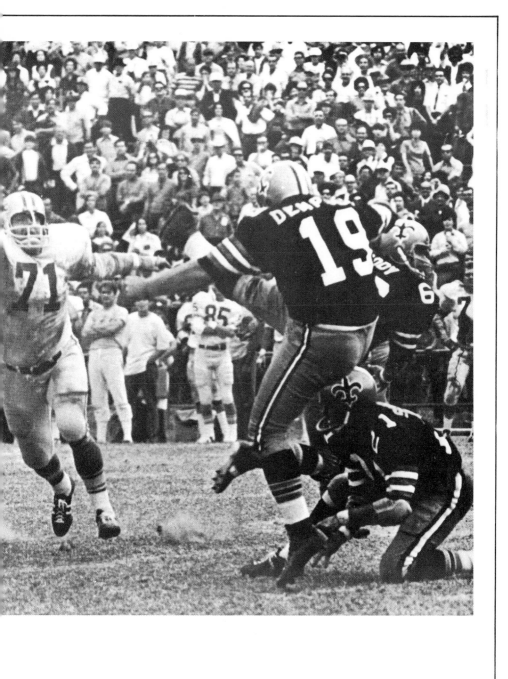

if it were jet-propelled, then soars . . . and soars . . . and soars. With the ball still in the air, the gun sounds ending the game . . . and then the unearthly kick sails between the uprights and over the crossbar—*by a good three yards!* It is incredible, utterly incredible. Tom Dempsey has broken the record for pro football's longest field goal, and broken it by plenty. And he has done it on the final play of the game, with time expired, giving a 19–17 victory to his underdog team and new coach. It is absurd, it is unbelievable, it is unprecedented.

It is, simply, the most dramatic finish to any game in pro-football history.

SCORING

LIONS	0	7	7	3 — 17
SAINTS	3	3	3	10 — 19

N.O.: Dempsey, FG, 29.
Det.: Farr, 10, run (Mann, kick).
N.O.: Dempsey, FG, 27.
Det.: Sanders, 2, pass from Munson (Mann, kick).
N.O.: Dempsey, FG, 8.
N.O.: Barrington, 4, run (Dempsey, kick).
Det.: Mann, FG, 18.
N.O.: Dempsey, FG, 63.

TEAM STATISTICS

	Lions	Saints
First downs	18	15
Rushing yardage	135	131
Passing yardage	143	141
Punt return yardage	14	14
Passes	13-25	16-28
Interceptions by	0	3
Punts	3-31	6-44
Fumbles lost	3	0
Yards penalized	31	124

INDIVIDUAL STATISTICS

RUSHES—Det.: Farr, 15 for 55 yards; Taylor, 16 for 55; Landry, 3 for 20; Munson, 1 for 5. N.O.: Otis, 18 for 70; Barrington, 15 for 61.

PASSES—Det.: Munson, 10 of 19 for 122 yards; Landry, 3 of 6 for 36. N.O.: Kilmer, 16 of 28 for 141.

RECEPTIONS—Det.: Sanders, 6 for 88 yards; McCullouch, 3 for 34; Walton, 3 for 32; Taylor, 1 for 4. N.O.: Abramowicz, 6 for 77; Barrington, 4 for 6; Otis, 3 for 26; Poage, 2 for 15; Dodd, 1 for 17.

December 21, 1974

MIAMI
DOLPHINS
VS.
OAKLAND
RAIDERS

Super Bowl VII is still three weeks away, but everyone is calling today's AFC divisional playoff "the real Super Bowl," for it matches the regular season's two finest teams: the defending-champion Miami Dolphins and the perennial-challenger Oakland Raiders. The widespread presumption is that whichever team wins this game will waltz through its remaining two opponents and attain pro-football supremacy. In truth, things will not work out that way—neither the Raiders nor the Dolphins will make it to the Super Bowl—but this contest will more than live up to its advance billing.

The Miami Dolphins came into being in 1966 and in the next few years they were dreadful, which was pretty much par for the expansion-team course. Then in 1970 Don Shula came over from Baltimore, and the Dolphins, who had gone 3–10–1 the season before, leaped to 10–4 and made the playoffs. The next year they reached the Super Bowl, where they lost to Dallas. And the year after that, 1972, they accomplished a first in NFL history: an undefeated, untied season, capped off by a triumph in the Super Bowl. The Dolphin winning streak was broken in the second game of the 1973 season—by Oakland—but Miami was still the class of the league, and rolled to another Super Bowl victory.

This year Miami opened the campaign fractured by dissension. Three of its key offensive players—fullback Larry Csonka, halfback Jim Kiick, and receiver Paul Warfield—signed contracts to play in the new World Football League in 1975. Nonetheless, all three contributed to the Dolphins' fourth consecutive AFC East crown, aided greatly by the men who were being groomed to replace them: fullback Don Nottingham, halfback Benny Malone, and receiver Nat Moore.

Miami bears the Shula stamp of an opportunistic, big-play defense and a methodical, ball-control offense. The Dolphins run the ball twice as often as they throw it; in their 1973 AFC championship confrontation with Oakland, for example, they won easily with quarterback Bob Griese passing only six times.

Oakland, on the other hand, has never been reluctant to air out the ball, from the mad bombing of Daryle Lamonica to the pinpoint precision of its current field leader, Kenny "the Snake" Stabler. And Oakland's high road to success has been very nearly as efficient as Miami's low road. From 1967 through 1974, the Raiders have produced pro football's best record, 84–21–7, while winning their division title each year but one. And yet in that time they made it to the Super Bowl only once (and lost), and now they find themselves saddled with the irksome reputation formerly held by Dallas: The Team That Can't Win The Big One.

Coach John Madden's outfit scored 25 points per game, more than any other team in this defense-dominated season in NFL history. And it wasn't all Stabler's aerial act, either—the Raiders' powerful running game produced more yards than anybody except the Steelers. Defending against the run was another matter, as the Dolphins demonstrated in last year's title game, when they racked up 266 rushing yards against Oakland; and this season the Raiders posted the AFC's worst record against the run. Yet looking at the bottom line, only two teams managed to outpoint the Raiders in a game all year—so how bad can the defense be?

Perhaps because the game is being played at the Oakland-Alameda County Stadium rather than the Orange Bowl, the Raiders are slight favorites to end the Dolphin dynasty on this dank and dreary Saturday.

Booting for Oakland is George Jakowenko, a specialist among specialists: With the forty-six-year-old George Blanda still on the scene to try from placement but unable any longer to boom kickoffs into the end zone, Jakowenko's job is strictly to kick off—which he does, to Nat Moore at the 11-yard line. A rookie drafted from Florida who has exceeded all expectations to become the team's top receiver, Moore rockets through Oakland's wall of defenders at the left side and breaks into the clear. While many patrons are still locating their seats, Moore, wearing number 89, races 89 yards to the touchdown!

Garo Yepremian kicks the extra point to give Miami a 7–0 lead fifteen seconds into the game. His holder, by the way, is Earl Morrall. He has played little this season as Griese's backup, but in recent years has done a great deal to make up for the disappointment of his Super Bowl loss to the Jets. In 1970 he was backup to Johnny Unitas during the regular season, then relieved him in the Super Bowl and directed the Colts to victory.

In 1972 he moved over to Miami and, when Griese was injured in midseason, stepped in to continue the Dolphins' unbeaten streak and win a second MVP award. Now forty years old, Earl is still two years shy of closing out a remarkable career as the game's greatest relief pitcher.

Yepremian kicks off to the Oakland 11, but return man Harold Hart cannot retaliate with an eighty-nine-yard dash of his own: He is brought down at the 31. Oakland's black-and-silver-clad offense is led out by Kenny Stabler, like Starr and Namath a product of Bear Bryant's University of Alabama. In his second year as a starter after bumping Lamonica to the bench, Kenny is a left-hander with an extremely compact throwing motion that produced twenty-six touchdowns this year, a league high. Behind him are fullback Marv Hubbard, who emerged from unlikely Colgate to become the team's leading rusher in each of the last four years; and Clarence Davis, a small, shifty speedster who provides the outside threat. At one wide receiver is Fred Biletnikoff, sure-handed and slow like Raymond Berry and who, like Berry, will go on to catch forty or more passes in ten straight seasons. The other wide receiver is Cliff Branch, a world-class sprinter who earned a full-time job this year only because the regular was injured, then went on to lead the league in touchdown catches and yardage. Tight end Bob Moore is a clutch pass-catcher who will hang on to the ball over the middle.

The offensive line is equally adept at blocking for Stabler or firing out for the run. The left side is manned by all-pros Gene Upshaw and Art Shell; the right side by George Buehler and John Vella; and the center by "Old 00" (the number on his jersey), Jim Otto, an original Raider from the inception of the AFL back in 1960.

Trying to stop this arsenal is Miami's "no-name defense," a term that may have described the unit aptly a few years ago but certainly does not today. What football fan has never heard such names as Nick Buoniconti, Dick Anderson, Jake Scott, Bill Stanfill?

Stabler's first call is a give to Davis, who slithers up the middle for four yards. He is stopped by left linebacker Bob Matheson, whose jersey number 53 gave name to Miami's celebrated "53 defense," a prevent alignment in which Matheson (or some other linebacker) would replace a down-lineman. The next two hand-offs go to Hubbard, who bulls for the first down at the Raider 42. Stabler is sticking to his game plan, which is to establish the run and thus inhibit Miami's mobile linebackers from taking deep drops into the passing lanes.

On second down and eight Stabler drops back to try his first pass, to Branch cutting over the middle twenty yards downfield. But the timing of the pattern is off; safety Dick Anderson intercepts at the 34 and returns the ball eighteen yards. Only three minutes into the game, Oakland already finds itself in a critical situation.

Now let's have a look at the Dolphins' offensive unit. At quarterback is Bob Griese, an excellent field general through Miami's gruesome years as well as its great ones; he is a reliable middle-distance passer despite being legally blind in one eye. At fullback is the huge Larry Csonka who, in the classic mold of Bronko Nagurski, prefers to run over people rather than around them. The speed is supplied by halfback Benny Malone, a rookie who beat out veterans Jim Kiick and Mercury Morris for the starting spot. The wide receiver opposite from Nat Moore is Paul Warfield, one of the great long-ball threats ever to play the game, but past his peak at the age of thirty-one. The tight end, playing in place of starter Jim Mandich, is veteran Marv Fleming; like Morrall, he has led an exceedingly charmed life, having played in two Super Bowls with the Packers and three more with the Dolphins. And the offensive line is a great one, perhaps the single finest component of the club, with four of its five starters having earned all-pro recognition.

In each of the three seasons before this one, Larry Csonka gained over 1,000 yards and was named the AFC's top fullback. In 1974, however, his performance has slipped, perhaps because of worries surrounding his impending move to the World Football League.

Griese's first-down play from the Miami 48 is a handoff to Csonka, who barges over left tackle for three. Fifteen yards more are tacked on for an Oakland personal foul. But here, at its own 34, Oakland draws the line. Malone and Csonka each try the middle with scant results, and on third and fourteen following a Miami penalty, Griese's long pass to Warfield in the end zone falls incomplete.

With fourth and fourteen from the 38, you might expect Yepremian to try a forty-five-yard field goal. But this is the year that the goalposts have been pushed back to the rear of the end zone, where they haven't been since 1932, in an effort to stem the flood of field goals and encourage touchdowns. The more noticeable effect of this change, however, has been to encourage punters to kick for the coffin corner, denying the fans a chance to see a runback. Miami's punter, Larry Seiple, lifts a soft twenty-five-yarder out of bounds at the 13.

Stabler lets Davis and Hubbard move the ball out beyond the shadow of Oakland's goalposts for a first down at the 25. But now his trigger finger begins to itch: he sends Branch deep down the left sideline and slings one as far as he can, some sixty yards in the air . . . incomplete, but it should have the intended effect of loosening up the coverage underneath. On the next play Stabler hits Biletnikoff for fifteen yards to the 40. He manages one more short completion to Branch, but at the 49 the drive stalls. In comes Ray Guy, the best punter in recent memory. He booms a beauty toward the coffin corner, but it just nicks the airspace over the end zone before sailing out of bounds.

The Dolphins take over at the 20, resuming their ground-oriented assault. Five straight running plays position the ball at the Miami 46, and then, on first down, Griese throws to Moore at the left sideline to the 37. The Dolphins are knocking at the door again; but again an inopportune penalty helps Oakland bar the door. On third down and ten, Griese goes to Warfield at the right sideline, where the pass is knocked down by Nemiah Wilson. Seiple comes on to try the angled kick; as Guy did, he cuts it too fine and catches a part of the end zone. Wouldn't you rather have seen George Blanda try a field goal from the 44?

After another exchange of punts, Oakland resumes possession at its 22, three minutes into the second period. Frustrated by his inability to move even as far as midfield, Stabler goes to the air on first down and connects with Biletnikoff for nine. Hubbard charges up the middle for five, then grabs another first-down toss from Stabler. This change in tempo seems to be working. On second and one, Davis bolts through the line and into the secondary, where Curtis Johnson chases him down after a gain of nineteen. Oakland is now in Dolphin territory, at the 36, and in high gear. On third and five, following two rushes, reserve running back Charley Smith floats downfield; with the wide receivers occupying the deep backs, the only man he has to beat is middle linebacker Nick Buoniconti. He outruns Buoniconti all the way to the end zone, where Stabler's pass finds him. The fans erupt—this is the team they know, not that timid bunch of the opening period, masquerading as the Raiders! Blanda's extra point ties the score at 7.

Hubert Ginn returns the kickoff to the 37. Will the Dolphins open up a bit now? Remember, it wasn't the offense that provided their touchdown. But Shula is not yet convinced that Oakland can stop the run, and he knows that when you put the ball in the air only three things can happen and two of those are bad. On first down Malone jets up the middle for eleven, forcing Jack Tatum to come up and make the stop. Csonka follows right guard Larry Little and right tackle Norm Evans for a gain of six, then Kiick takes the same route for two, and Csonka comes back for nine more. Otis Sistrunk and Bubba Smith, the left side of the Oakland line, know what's coming but are powerless to do anything about it.

The drive continues as, on a third and four from the Raider 29, Griese tosses out in the flat to Kiick for five. Then, trying to cross up the Raiders, Griese fires to Moore down the right

Charley Smith beats Nick Buoniconti in a race for the ball, as a back generally does when he goes one-on-one against a linebacker. Buoniconti's coverage is excellent, but the pass from Kenny Stabler is better. Oakland ties up the game.

sideline—incomplete. Placed in an obvious passing situation, Griese tries to outsmart Oakland again with a draw to Csonka, but Horace Jones wraps up Zonk for a loss of one. There'll be no deception now. Griese fades and, finding no one open, swings out a pass to short, squat Don Nottingham, the "human bowling ball," who rolls downfield to the 16, two yards shy of the first down. Only 1:04 remains in the half, which has flown by very quickly because of all the running plays. Garo Yepremian, the soccer-style kicker from Cyprus, boots a thirty-three-yard field goal to give Miami the 10–7 lead it will take into the locker room at halftime.

How shall we judge the first half? That it was no masterpiece and—dare we say it—more than a little boring? Coaches love to play boring football, because that means they are taking the least amount of risk required to win. In order to win, they know, you must first keep from losing: turn the ball over as little as possible, keep the ball in your own hands as long as possible, and let the clock work for you when you have the lead. The "exciting" game which fans love and coaches despise often features a rash of turnovers and blunders and produces scoring in bundles. The great game can blossom from the boring one as the clock runs down on the second half, as the trailing team strays more and more from its game plan and ultimately casts it aside, playing to win the way the fans would like to see them play all the time. That's what's in store for us.

Hart returns Yepremian's opening kickoff to the 29. Stabler, who quietly completed eight of twelve passes for ninety-four net yards in the first half, takes to the air on first down. At least, he tries to, but is run out of the pocket by Manny Fernandez, who brings him down for a loss of three. Davis then sweeps left for nine, but Branch drops a third-down pass. Guy sends a forty-four-yard punt to the 21, where Nat Moore catches it and is immediately slammed to earth.

Will Griese be any more daring? His first-half stats show three completions in six attempts, for the grand total of twenty-one yards. But it's Csonka for three, Csonka for three more, a bad pass, and a punt.

The Raiders resume possession at their 40. Right off the bat, Stabler hits Biletnikoff for twenty yards. Coach Madden has uncoiled the Snake, and the fans are ecstatic. On the next play Stabler goes for it all to Biletnikoff, who is well covered in the end zone by reserve safety Charlie Babb, in for the injured Jake Scott. The pass is incomplete, but reestablishes the deep threat in the minds of the secondary men.

Clarence Davis gains three behind the block of Gene Upshaw. On third and seven at the Miami 37, Biletnikoff and Branch are both double-covered, so Stabler looks to Bob Moore over the middle and connects for the necessary yardage. An incompletion to Biletnikoff is followed by a handoff to Pete Banaszak, who slants off right guard George Buehler's fine block for nine big yards. With Miami looking for a fullback plunge on third and one, Stabler hands to Davis, who slips through a crack off the left side for eight.

The stadium is alive now—with Stabler moving the team through the air, suddenly the running game has begun to function more smoothly too. On second down Stabler throws his fourth pass of the drive to Biletnikoff, in the right corner of the end zone. Touchdown! Blanda converts, and Oakland takes the lead for the first time in the game, 14–10.

Not for long, as it turns out. On third and seven at the Oakland 45, Griese throws a bomb to Jim Kiick, racing downfield stride for stride with linebacker Phil Villapiano. But as the ball descends, so does a yellow flag—interference against the linebacker, giving Miami a first down at the Oakland 16. While the Raiders are still confounded by the previous play, Griese comes right back with a touchdown pass to Warfield. Now comes a potentially crucial miscue: Yepremian's PAT is low, and the six-foot-seven-inch Bubba Smith breaks through to smother it. The score stands at 16–14.

More than six and a half minutes remain in the quarter, but both teams act as if they had spent their energies in recording their touchdowns. Oakland runs through two futile possessions, in which the Dolphin line places increasing pressure on Stabler. Miami, despite good field position, returns to its dreary format of running on the first two downs and then looking for a miracle on third and long.

On the last play of the quarter Miami, having just taken possession at the 19, again sends Csonka up the middle on first down—but this time Zonk breaks through for fifteen. Having to defend against the run, down after down, all afternoon, may be taking its toll on the Oakland front four. Malone follows with a right-end sweep for seven, and then Csonka picks up the first down. If the Dolphins can continue to run like this, why bother to pass? But on a brilliant call at this juncture, Griese freezes the linebackers with a fake to the middle, then turns and drills a pass to Warfield at the left sideline for twenty.

Malone and Csonka move the ball to the Raider 28, confronting Griese with a third and three. You'd figure him for a run, wouldn't you? Oakland does, but Griese flips a pass out to Warfield, open at the left sideline—and the impeccable receiver drops it. Yepremian comes on to try a forty-six-yard field goal, just at the edge of his effective range. Though he has kicked them longer on occasion, Garo is more prized for his accuracy inside the 40 than for his ability to hit an occasional whopper. This kick is good, lifting Miami's lead to 19–14.

Oakland takes over at the 39 following a fine kickoff return by Hart, but meets with failure again. There's still plenty of time left—10:11, to be exact—but the fans are starting to squirm in their seats. It's been a while since the Raiders have done anything on offense, and their defense seems "out of synch" with Miami's play selection. What Oakland needs is a break—a timely turnover or penalty or defensive blunder—but the Dolphins are not likely to give it to them. Like the Packers of Vince Lombardi, Shula's Dolphins are masters of execution who don't beat themselves.

Taking over at the 20 after Guy's punt dribbles into the end zone, Miami trudges back up the field. Csonka. Malone. Csonka. First down. Zonk gains three more to place the ball at the 34, then Griese throws a safe little pass to Warfield at the left sideline for the first down. These hit-and-run air strikes are infuriatingly difficult to stop. But on third and seven at the Miami 48, Griese declines to throw: He sends Malone around right end, where he is stopped one yard short of the first. Did Bob simply make a wrong guess in his cat-and-mouse game with the Oakland defenders, or was he trying to sit on a lead? In any event, while moving forward only thirty-six yards, Miami has succeeded in consuming more than five minutes' playing time.

Seiple once again flubs the coffin-corner kick, allowing Oakland to start from its 17. There is 4:54 left in the game. The fans beg their heroes to do something heroic before it is too late. On first down Stabler, filled with more of a sense of urgency, goes to Biletnikoff for eleven. And then he goes deep, sending Branch speeding down the left sideline against Henry Stuckey, a reserve cornerback who has had to replace the injured Curtis Johnson. (Losing both Jake Scott and Johnson in the same game is tough luck against an offense like this.) Stabler underestimates Branch's speed and underthrows the pass—but Cliff, who has dropped some catchable balls earlier, dives to make a marvelous grab at the 27. Stuckey, catching up from behind, skids past the fallen Branch—*but doesn't touch him*. Knowing that the play is not dead until he *is* touched, Branch scrambles up and resumes his course down the left sideline for the touchdown! Miami players protest feebly, but the points are already up on the board. Blanda's kick makes the score 21–19. This touchdown "drive" consumed all of seventeen seconds.

Hubert Ginn returns the kickoff to the Miami 32. With 4:28 on the clock, Griese comes out firing. His first-down pass to Nat Moore is good for twenty-three yards. Hit . . . and run—Csonka rolls around right end for seven, led by the incomparable Larry Little. Then back to the trenches: Csonka bursts over the middle. Knocking defenders down like so many matchsticks, he gains fifteen yards to the Raider 23. Under two and a half minutes to play; a field goal will give Miami the lead. The Raiders brace for another blast up the middle, but Griese sends a short pitch back to Malone, who sweeps right end. Spinning away from some tacklers, bouncing off others, and nearly stepping out of bounds several times, the rookie tightropes his way up the sideline, all the way into the end zone! Yepremian's kick makes the score Miami 26, Oakland 21.

This drive has been a tremendous display of performance under pressure. If Shula has any complaint, it can only be that the touchdown was scored too quickly. As Yepremian kicks off to Ron Smith, 2:08 remains to be played, an eternity for a quarterback like Stabler. On the other hand, Miami's prevent defense is mighty tough to beat in the closing moments, especially when it takes a touchdown rather than a field goal to win.

On first down Stabler sees that Branch and Biletnikoff are covered, so he checks off to Moore for six yards, to the 38. The two-minute warning is given. Next Oakland tries to trap Miami's tackles, sending Davis into the middle, but Manny Fernandez "stays home": The play gains only one. Now Stabler finds himself in a crucial third and three, so he goes to Biletnikoff. Freddy makes the catch and whirls upfield for eighteen yards to the Miami 43. Timeout is called.

With the secondary overplaying to the outside, figuring that Oakland will try to conserve precious seconds with sideline patterns, Stabler crosses them up. Biletnikoff runs downfield from the right flank, gives a little shake-and-bake move to Tim Foley, and turns his route into the middle. The pass is right there, and he catches it in front of Dick Anderson for a gain of twenty! Exactly one minute remains, and Oakland has the ball on the 23 with two timeouts left.

The Raiders hurry to the new line of scrimmage—in the huddle following the timeout, Stabler had relayed the next two plays to be used. This time Kenny does look to the sideline, the left sideline where Miami misses Scott and Johnson, and hits Branch. Cliff gains four, but more important, he gets out of bounds to stop the clock. Now Frank Pitts, a ten-year veteran who has caught only one pass all year (and that for a loss of ten), enters the lineup for Branch, and snares a five-yarder. Linebacker Bob Matheson prevents him from racing out of bounds, so the Raiders must use another timeout. Only forty seconds remain, and they confront a third down and one at the 14.

Stabler and Madden discuss the alternatives. If they pass, to save the timeout, and miss, then the entire season will hang on the next play. If they run, and fail to make the first down, they will have to use their final timeout and in all probability pass on fourth down. If they run and do make the first down, they can call their final timeout and still have time enough for four—if necessary—pass attempts.

Shouting his signals over the bedlam roar of the crowd, Stabler takes the snap from Jim Otto, spins, and slams the ball into the abdomen of Clarence Davis. The halfback slips outside, then cuts in behind the crunching blocks of Shell and Upshaw for a gain of six. The last timeout is called. Thirty-five seconds show on the clock.

In the huddle, Stabler calls a play for Biletnikoff, who has already caught eight passes for 122 yards. Fred will juke inside, then cut for the right corner of the end zone. Tight end Bob Moore will stay on the line to block, hoping to draw the linebackers up a step in anticipation of a run, then drift downfield over the middle as a secondary receiver. Moore's fake, if it works,

Benny Malone has sidestepped a stream of would-be Raider tacklers on his journey to the end zone, and now eludes the final one. All Miami must do is protect its five-point lead for two more minutes.

will make it easier for Davis and Hubbard to get into the pass pattern, too.

That is how it's supposed to work (see diagram). But as Stabler fades to pass, Moore's fake fools no one—seven defenders drop back—and Biletnikoff is blanketed. Drifting to his left, looking for someone to get open, Stabler suddenly feels his legs being pulled out from under him! Vern Den Herder has circled around from the opposite end of the line to lock his arms around Kenny's ankles.

Clarence Davis, seeing that Stabler is in a fix, comes back toward his quarterback from deep in the end zone. The Snake cannot wriggle free of his pursuer and, as he falls forward, spots Davis at the last instant and wrists a floater in his direction. The five-foot-ten-inch Davis is surrounded by taller, heftier Dolphins as he leaps for the ball. Somehow he gets his hands on it, but so does linebacker Mike Kolen, who outweighs Davis by thirty pounds. Summoning up some unknown strength, Davis wrests the ball away as he falls in the end zone—touchdown!

Blanda adds the meaningless point as the jubilant crowd stomps and cheers. But there are twenty-six seconds left, and the Dolphins can still win with a field goal.

Moore returns the kickoff to the 33, and then Griese's short pass is intercepted by Villapiano. Three Marv Hubbard rushes take care of the clock. The Dolphin rule is over, and the Raiders have won the big one at last. Capturing the Super Bowl is a foregone conclusion.

The euphoria will last only through the week, until the Pittsburgh Steelers burst Oakland's balloon on *their* way to the Super Bowl and a dynasty of their own. The Raiders? They will have to wait for 1977 to wear Super Bowl rings. But their victory in today's "real Super Bowl" will resonate in the memories of all those who witnessed it, long after all but a few Super Bowls are forgotten.

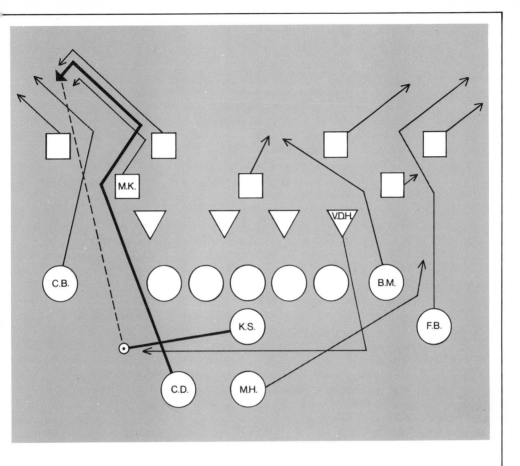

*A broken play provides the touchdown. When Kenny Stabler (K.S.)
sees that his primary receiver, Fred Biletnikoff (F.B.), is double-
covered, he looks to Bob Moore (B.M.). But Moore is blanketed, too,
so Stabler shoots a glance at Marv Hubbard (M.H.) in the right flat.
Hubbard cannot shake free, either, so Kenny deserts his crumbling
pocket and rolls left, pursued from behind by Vern Den Herder
(V.D.H.). Cliff Branch (C.B.) and Clarence Davis (C.D.) are both in
the same area of the left end zone, compromising each other's mobil-
ity and simplifying the coverage. As Den Herder grabs Stabler, Davis
comes back toward the line, trying to provide a target. Desperately,
Stabler flips the ball to him, despite the fact that linebacker Mike
Kolen (M.K.) is right there, too. Kolen and Davis wrestle for the ball;
somehow Davis comes away with it. It's not pretty, but it's six points
all the same.*

SCORING

DOLPHINS	7	3	6	10 — 26
RAIDERS	0	7	7	14 — 28

Mia.: N. Moore, 89, kickoff return (Yepremian, kick).
Oak.: C. Smith, 31, pass from Stabler (Blanda, kick).
Mia.: Yepremian, FG, 33.
Oak.: Biletnikoff, 13, pass from Stabler (Blanda, kick).
Mia.: Warfield, 16, pass from Griese (kick blocked).
Mia.: Yepremian, FG, 46.
Oak.: Branch, 72, pass from Stabler (Blanda, kick).
Mia.: Malone, 23, run (Yepremian, kick).
Oak.: Davis, 8, pass from Stabler (Blanda, kick).

TEAM STATISTICS

	Dolphins	Raiders
First downs	18	19
Rushing yardage	213	135
Passing yardage	81	276
Punt return yardage	5	16
Passes	7-14	20-30
Interceptions by	1	1
Punts	6-33	7-43
Fumbles lost	0	0
Yards penalized	15	59

INDIVIDUAL STATISTICS

RUSHES—Mia.: Csonka, 24 for 114 yards; Malone, 14 for 83; Griese, 2 for 14; Kiick, 1 for 2. Oak.: Hubbard, 14 for 55; Davis, 12 for 59; Banaszak, 3 for 14; Stabler, 3 for 7.

PASSES—Mia.: Griese, 7 of 14 for 101 yards. Oak.: Stabler, 20 of 30 for 293.

RECEPTIONS—Mia.: Warfield, 3 for 47 yards; N. Moore, 2 for 40; Nottingham, 1 for 9; Kiick, 1 for 5. Oak.: Biletnikoff, 8 for 122; Branch, 3 for 84; B. Moore, 3 for 22; C. Smith, 2 for 35; Davis, 2 for 16; Hubbard, 1 for 9; Pitts, 1 for 5.

December 16, 1979

WASHINGTON REDSKINS

VS.

DALLAS COWBOYS

Twelve years ago, when we came in from the cold of Green Bay's Lambeau Stadium, we left behind a despondent Dallas Cowboy team that, for the second time in a row, had seen a championship snatched from its grasp in the final seconds. Yet in the years since that frozen epic, while the noble Packers declined and other "dynasties" came and went, the Cowboys kept on winning. Since 1966 Tom Landry's personnel has turned over completely, yet his team has made the playoffs every year but one and participated in five Super Bowls—quite a tribute to his coaching system.

177

Right on the Cowboys' heels throughout the 1970s have been their bitter rivals, the Washington Redskins. Vince Lombardi had turned Redskin fortunes around in 1969, his first and only year as their mentor, just as he had done at Green Bay a decade earlier. But Lombardi's untimely death in September 1970 left the franchise in disarray until George Allen took over the reins the following season. Relying on veterans deemed too old by other teams, Allen brought success to the capital. Four times the Redskins made the playoffs as a wild-card entry, and one time they beat out Dallas and went on to the Super Bowl.

One of the "Over-the-Hill Gang" from that 1973 Super Bowl team, linebacker Jack Pardee, took over for Allen in 1978 and got off to a 6–0 start—but then the veterans crumbled all at once, losing eight of their last ten. This year, with the coach committing himself to inject youth into the team, most experts picked Washington to finish no higher than fourth in their division. But Pardee has blended his remaining geezers into the youth movement with considerable skill and, as the Redskins and Cowboys get ready to square off in Texas Stadium, on this last Sunday of the regular season, first place in the NFC East waits on the outcome.

The playoff picture, modified last year to include four wild-card contestants, is extremely complicated and, for the Redskins, crucial. Coming into this final Sunday, Washington, Dallas, and the Philadelphia Eagles all have records of 10–5. Dallas and Philadelphia, however, can lose today and still be assured wild-card status. The Redskins, on the other hand, must win to be guaranteed a playoff spot. If they lose, everything will depend on what Chicago does in its game against St. Louis. If the Bears win that game to bring their record to 10–6, the NFL will apply a controversial standard called "point differential" to determine whether the Bears or the Redskins enter postseason play.

Point differential is simply the difference between the total points a team scores during the season and the points it allows.

Through the first fifteen weeks, Washington has scored 54 points more than its opponents, while Chicago's point differential stands at only 21. Thus if Washington were to lose to the Cowboys today by, say, 7 points, the Bears would have to defeat the Cardinals by at least 27 to nail down the wild card. (The last time point differential decided a playoff spot was in 1977, when the Redskins were beaten out by the Bears—who were then coached by Pardee!)

The Redskins defeated Dallas in Washington last month, enraging Cowboy partisans by tacking on a final-minute field goal to an insurmountable lead. Pardee may have felt he was innocently building up his point differential, but Dallas accused him of simply rubbing it in—particularly since two weeks later, in a wipeout of Green Bay, the Redskins disdained to go for a closing touchdown they might easily have scored. Anyway, with these teams' history of hard-fought battles there is no need to conjure up extra motivation. More than 62,000 fans are whooping it up already on this blustery, gray afternoon.

And here we go—the kickoff descends to Ron Springs, a fifth-round Dallas draft choice who will replace the injured star, Tony Dorsett, in the backfield today. The nervous rookie fields the bounding ball, fumbles, and then falls on it at the 22. Out comes the offensive unit, led by thirty-seven-year-old Roger Staubach, the NFL's top-ranked passer this year and one of the all-time greats. He will be attacking an erratic Redskin defense that gives up a lot of yardage but has a knack for producing turnovers.

On first down, trying to settle Springs into the rhythm of the game, Staubach swings a pass to him for five yards. On second down a handoff also goes to Springs, who gains four behind right guard Tom Rafferty . . . but fumbles again. This time the ball does not bounce back to him; linebacker Brad Dusek recovers at the Dallas 34.

Now the Redskins are in ideal position to jump out in front.

Roger Staubach is the on-field maestro of Tom Landry's multiple offense, and a magician in the two-minute drill.

Their thirty-one-year-old quarterback, Joe Theismann, has matured into an outstanding field leader this season, after several years as a backup to ancient Bill Kilmer. In the backfield with him are Benny Malone, whom you will remember in a Miami uniform, and John Riggins, a dangerous runner who combines the strength of a fullback with the speed of a scatback. The receivers are rookie tight end Don Warren and wide men Danny Buggs and Ricky Thompson; all are competent, none is outstanding. The same might be said of the offensive line, whose job of pass protection is made easier by Theismann's ability to scramble.

This unit will be facing a Dallas defense riddled by injury and controversy: Safeties Charley Waters and Randy Hughes are banged up and out of action; defensive tackle Randy White is playing on a bad ankle; linebacker Tom "Hollywood" Henderson was released in midseason for clowning on the bench during a losing contest; and defensive end "Too Tall" Jones gave up football to try his hand at boxing. The result of all this has been a mediocre pass rush and a sometimes confused secondary.

Moving haltingly toward the Dallas goal, Washington gets a lift from reserve back Ike Forte. He comes in for Malone in a third-and-three situation at the 27 and runs for the necessary yardage, then converts a third and ten with a safety-valve pass all the way to the 9. Riggins takes two cracks at running it in and Theismann tries to pass it in, but Dallas stands firm. Mark Moseley, one of the few remaining straight-on kickers in football, comes in to boot a twenty-four-yard field goal.

Starting from its 30 after the kickoff, Dallas picks up two first downs and moves into Washington territory. On first down at the 45, Staubach passes over the middle for Tony Hill, the team's leading receiver this year, but linebacker Neal Olkewicz drops back to tip it away. On second and ten Landry's call is a draw to the squat fullback, Robert Newhouse, who is stopped at the line—and fumbles! Again, Dusek is there to recover.

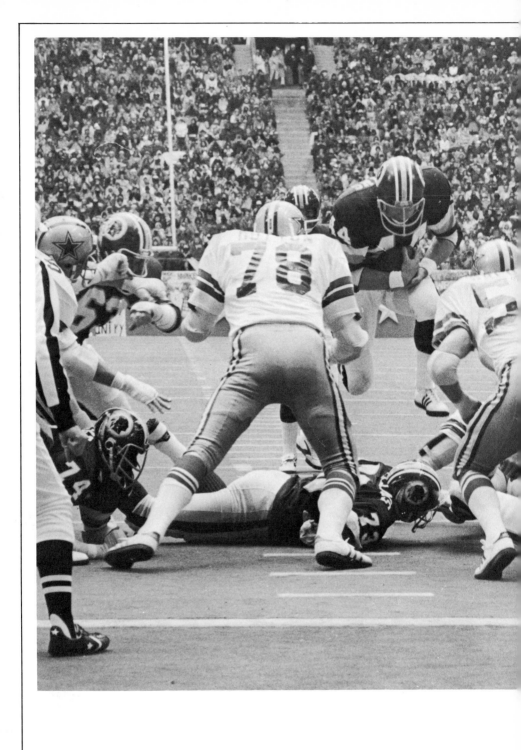

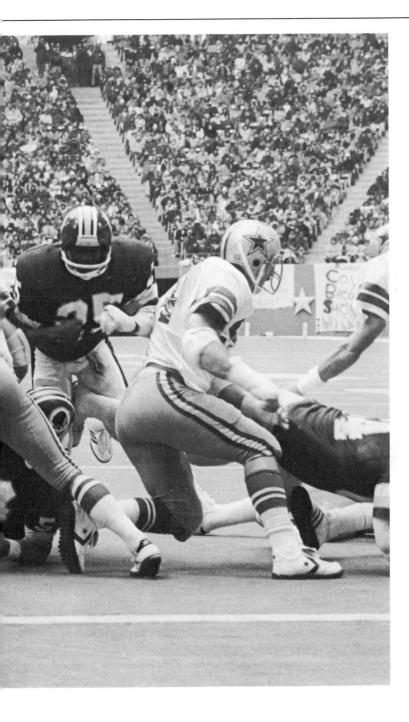

In the Redskins' opening series, John Riggins goes airborne at the 4-yard line, but the hole is about to close. John Dutton (78) and Bob Breunig (53) rack Riggins up at the 3.

Just as in the two Dallas games we witnessed back in 1967, the Cowboys are digging themselves into a hole from which they may not be able to climb out.

Immediately Theismann goes deep to Danny Buggs, who has beaten cornerback Aaron Kyle. Danny makes the catch at the 25 and runs for another seven before free safety Cliff Harris hauls him down. The play is good for thirty-nine yards to the 18. Now Riggins takes a handoff and rumbles behind a fine block by right tackle George Starke for fourteen more. A personal foul against Dallas halves the distance to the goal line, and a sweep by Malone halves it again. From the 1, Theismann rolls in for the score. The Dallas natives are getting restless.

Are the Cowboys ready to wake up now that they are 10 points down? Starting from their 22, Staubach hands to Springs for four yards in the middle. Then his pass is batted down at the line, bringing up a third and six. Into the game comes Preston Pearson, a thirteen-year veteran whose specialty is outmaneuvering a linebacker to catch a vital third-down pass. And that's exactly what he does, snaring a twenty-six-yarder. Pearson, who returned kicks for Baltimore in the 1969 Super Bowl, is one of the very few players Landry has acquired from another club in the last decade; Dallas likes its Cowboys homegrown, but Preston has been adopted wholeheartedly.

With the ball at the Redskin 48, Springs and Newhouse rush for another first down. But at the 37, the drive stalls as on third down and ten Staubach misreads the coverage of the Washington secondary, thinking it to be in a zone when it is actually playing a man-to-man; the result is that he overthrows an open receiver. Danny White punts into the end zone, and the Redskins try to move out from their 20.

They don't, but after an exchange of punts by Washington's Mike Bragg and White, the Redskins resume possession at their 20 with eight seconds remaining in the period. Malone dives for two yards as the gun sounds. Dallas has had the ball for nine minutes compared to Washington's six, but Washington has 10 points to Dallas's none, and that's all that counts.

From the 22 Theismann finds Buggs again, for ten yards. The Dallas secondary, playing exclusively man-to-man, seems ripe for the picking, so Theismann fades to pass again. But big John Dutton, the six-foot-seven, 265-pound defensive end, storms through to dump Joe for a loss of eleven. Unfazed, he fades to pass again, and takes advantage of the strong Dallas charge with a flip to reserve fullback Clarence Harmon, who barrels past the linebackers for twenty yards to the Redskin 41. Riggins picks up the first down.

On second and eight from the Washington 45, Theismann looks to throw to a wide receiver—but then he spots Malone being covered one-on-one by linebacker D. D. Lewis. He throws to Malone at the Dallas 44; Benny gives Lewis a fake toward the middle, then blasts past him up the left sideline. The secondary gives chase, but Benny is gone—the fifty-five-yard TD is Washington's longest scoring play of the season.

There is no joy in Dallas at this moment, and the knowledge that a wild-card berth awaits the Cowboys even in defeat is little comfort. These are the despised Redskins, who now stand to do what no Redskin team has ever done—sweep the season series from Dallas. And with word coming in that the Bears lead the Cardinals 21–0 at the half, it seems clear that the Redskins will have to do just that.

Behind 17–0 only two minutes into the second quarter, Dallas must start showing some life. Springs takes Moseley's kickoff at the 13 and brings it back to the 30. Coolly, Landry and Staubach stick to their guns, opening with a handoff to Springs, who hits the left side for four yards. It is this side that figures to be more vulnerable to the run: the Cowboys have two Pro Bowlers at tackle and guard, Pat Donovan and Herbert Scott, going against Diron Talbert and Coy Bacon, who have twenty-five years' pro experience between them and are more effective against the pass.

Staubach comes back with a screen pass to Springs, whose run after the catch accounts for the whole fourteen-yard gain. Then Springs circles right end for five. Not even Dorsett sees this much action, down after down. Backup fullback Scott Laidlaw interrupts Springs's one-man show to take a pass for four, moving the ball to the Skin 43.

On third down and six at the 34, the Redskins insert a "nickel back," or fifth defensive back, and Monte Coleman, an exceptionally swift linebacker. Nonetheless, Staubach throws to Springs for ten yards and the first down. The crowd loves it. Newhouse bursts up the middle to the 16. The next four handoffs go to Springs, who caps the drive with a plunge over the left side for the score. Dallas has moved seventy yards in thirteen plays, ten of them involving Ron Springs, who doesn't seem nervous anymore. Rafael Septien provides the PAT. The lead is cut to 17–7.

Bobby Hammond returns Septien's kickoff to the 30. Although Riggins opens up the series with a nine-yard gain around right end, Washington pulls up short at the 48 as Theismann's third-down pass to Harmon fails. Bragg punts a thirty-seven-yard floater to Steve Wilson, who signals for a fair catch at the 15. With 1:48 to play in the half, and the best two-minute quarterback since Unitas, Dallas will certainly go to the air now. Fasten your seat belts.

Dropping back into the shotgun formation (see diagram), a not-so-distant cousin of the old single wing which floods the secondary with receivers, Staubach fires a first-down pass to Springs. It is dropped, but Staubach then pierces the prevent defense with a twenty-one-yard strike to Hill. Now Washington plays the aggressor: blitzing linebacker Monte Coleman knifes through to drop Roger for a loss of six. But this is merely an annoyance—with 1:20 to play, Staubach is a pig in grease. In the shotgun on every play now, Staubach hits Springs for nine, Hill for twelve and then thirteen, and Drew Pearson for twenty. In fifty-three seconds, he has moved his team fifty-four yards to the Washington 16. Standing alone as a tailback, Staubach

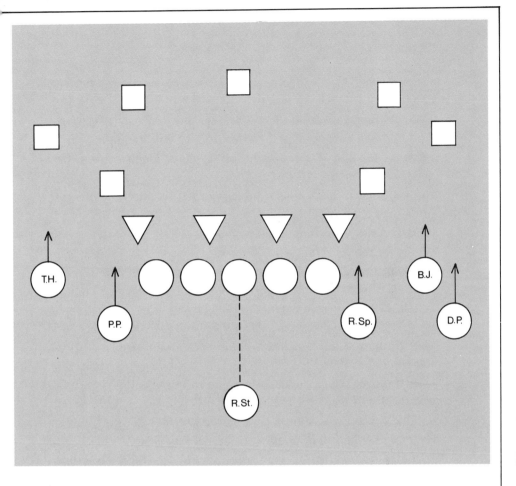

*The shotgun, invented by Red Hickey of the San Francisco 49ers in
1960, was the first pro deviation from the T in more than a decade.
Like its ancestors, the old wingback and short-punt formations, the
shotgun employs a tailback, who stands five to seven yards behind
the center and surveys his options more coolly than a T quarterback
could. The backs—for Dallas, Preston Pearson (P.P.) and Ron Springs
(R.S.)—are set out on the wings. The flanker, Drew Pearson (D.P.),
is positioned outside the "tight" end, Butch Johnson (B.J.), who in the
shotgun is actually split out just as wide as the "split" end, Tony Hill
(T.H.). While the defensive linemen huff and puff to reach tailback
Roger Staubach (R.S.), the receivers flood downfield against Washington's nickel defense. If the wide receivers are double-covered, that
leaves the other three in single coverage, a sure prescription for Redskin trouble should the pass rush fail.*

scans the field like a supermarket shopper reviewing the produce counters.

A holding call on Rafferty is a serious setback, costing the Cowboys ten yards which take them out of easy field-goal range. Incompletions to Hill and then Springs leave Dallas with a third and twenty on the 26. With fifteen seconds to play, Staubach still has time to hit a ten- to fifteen-yarder and stop the clock to bring the kicking team in.

Roger takes the snap and backpedals another few steps while surveying the receivers—no one is clearly open. But dashing for the goal line, Preston Pearson has a slight edge on Monte Coleman, who had picked him up just beyond the line of scrimmage, and is even with free safety Mark Murphy, who picks him up deep. The pass is arched perfectly between the defenders, and Pearson hangs on. Touchdown! Texas Stadium erupts as if this were the end of the game, not merely the end of the half. The momentum of the game has swung into the hands of the Cowboys, and the Redskins will have a hard time taking it back. Moments ago the Redskins had not a care on the horizon, but now, despite their 17–14 lead, they shuffle off the field dispiritedly.

In the second period Dallas was confronted with five third-down situations, and incredibly converted all five of them. This is the sign of a great quarterback, and that's just what Staubach has been in his eleven years with the Cowboys. He came to them as a twenty-six-year-old rookie after completing his service obligation to the Navy, with whom he had earned All-American honors. For a few years he played second fiddle to quarterback Craig Morton, then wrested the position away in mid-1971 and never gave it back. The melodramatic, come-from-behind victory became his signature, and his ticket to certain induction into the Hall of Fame.

The stadium is bathed in darkness as the teams return to the field for the second half. Septien's kick booms one yard deep into the end zone, where Hammond fields it and returns to the 18—but a clipping call means that the Redskin offense must start from the 9. Though Riggins and Theismann run the ball out to the 24, a Harvey Martin sack throws Washington back. On fourth down at the 21, Bragg slices the punt out of bounds at the Dallas 48, his third straight flub of the afternoon.

The fans greet their Cowboys with a roar, expecting them to pick up where they left off. The first three plays are rushes aimed at Bacon and Talbert, which yield a first down at the Washington 41. Having thus softened up the line, Staubach now goes to the air, hitting Hill on the left side for twelve. Washington's defense is tentative now, not knowing which way to turn. The Dallas version of the Ali shuffle continues, with wide receiver Butch Johnson, in for Hill, reversing into the backfield to take a handoff from Staubach and sweep right for thirteen more.

On first down from the 15, Hill cuts across the field and into the end zone, where he is covered tightly by Lemar Parrish; Staubach, feeling some pressure from the pass rush, wisely overthrows. Next, Springs gains four off the left side, bringing up a third down and six at the 11. In comes "Old Reliable," Preston Pearson, and Staubach shifts into the shotgun; the combination clicks again, down to the two. Newhouse cracks over the goal line behind Rafferty, Septien adds the point, and the Cowboys are in the driver's seat of a steamroller, though their lead is only 4 points.

Starting from the 24, the Redskins duplicate the pattern of their previous possession: they gain a first down on the ground, and then a sack—this time by Larry Cole—stops them dead in their tracks. Dallas is awesome right now; the Redskins need a break, and soon. In Chicago, where the kickoff time was earlier, the Bears have annihilated the Cardinals 42–6, wiping out the 33-point edge in point differential Washington held before today. It's no longer enough for the Redskins to stay close to

Dallas; if they are to make the playoffs, they must win.

Dallas starts from its 30 and goes with its workhorse, Springs, on the first two plays. But on third down and three, Perry Brooks breaks through to dump Staubach for a loss of ten. A flag has been thrown, undoubtedly for offensive holding, which Washington will reject . . . uh-oh, the call is *defensive* holding, against cornerback Parrish. It's an automatic first down for Dallas, and a horrible break for Washington.

But the Redskin defense shows a lot of heart, coming back on the field and holding the Cowboys to a gain of only one yard on the next three plays. Danny White is forced to punt, and he hits a beauty, forty-four yards and out of bounds at the 13. Only 1:36 remains in the third quarter.

Riggins powers over right tackle for five, then circles left end for seven more. Theismann tries his luck in the air again. He has yet to complete a pass in the period—in fact, he hasn't completed one since his touchdown to Malone at 1:53 into the *previous* period. But here the frustration ends—he hits a nine-yarder to John McDaniel, who has replaced Buggs. That unimpressive little completion may rekindle the pilot light of this languishing offense.

On third and one from the 34 Riggins bursts through the line for ten, thanks to a block by left guard Ron Saul. Then it's Riggins up the middle for four as the period ends. Moving upfield cautiously, the Redskins are mounting a nice little drive which is making the Dallas racehorses cool their heels. Theismann stays under control, flipping a screen pass to McDaniel for a first down, bootlegging around right end for another, and zipping the ball to Thompson at the 16 for the fifth first down of the series.

Now the Dallas defense will be put to the test. Malone hits the right side for three, then Riggins does for four—but on Riggins's run, Malone went forward before the snap, and the ball comes back to the 18 on the penalty. On second and twelve

Theismann swings a pass out to Harmon, who charges down to the 7 before Kyle and linebacker Guy Brown bring him down.

Third and one. What would you call? Riggins off tackle? Harmon up the middle? A quarterback sneak? With the Cowboys stacked up for the plunge into the line, Theismann fakes a handoff, spins, and sets up: daringly, he throws for Harmon in the end zone . . . but wide. Now do you go for 6 or settle for 3? Eleven and a half minutes remain, and Washington cannot bear to come away from this magnificent drive without any points. Pardee brings on Moseley, the NFC's leading scorer this year, to kick another twenty-four-yard field goal. The Dallas lead is shaved to 21–20.

On the kickoff the fired-up Redskin special team, which calls itself the Wild Bunch, nails Springs at the 14. Dallas tries to rein in the Skins' high spirits with a play-action pass on first down, but nobody is open; Staubach has to eat a one-yard loss. His second-down attempt to Drew Pearson misses. It's time now for Preston Pearson and the shotgun offense. The play that has been so successful today has been to send Pearson over the middle while the strong-side wide receiver runs his pattern downfield. Free safety Mark Murphy has been drifting over to back up the strong side, leaving Pearson covered by a linebacker. But this time Murphy smells the play coming, and overplays toward the middle. When the pass is airborne to Pearson at the 38, Murphy steps in front to intercept, and returns thirteen yards.

It's strange how fast a stadium can quiet. Sixty-two thousand people are here, and yet you can almost hear the whooping and hollering on the Washington sideline.

Theismann goes for the lead on his first play, lofting a long pass to Ricky Thompson in the end zone, where he is being played by Cliff Harris. The ball hangs a bit, and Harris has to decide whether to risk going for the interception or play it safe and bat it away. He chooses the latter—but down goes the yellow flag. Interference! Harris is irate, but the ball is on the Dallas 1, and Washington has four chances to ram it in.

One chance proves enough, as Riggins blasts over the right side for the score. Moseley's PAT puts the Redskins back in front, 27–21, with 10:18 to play.

Dallas does nothing in its next turn on offense, and White punts to the Redskin 31. Riggins struggles for three yards off the right side, which he has favored most of the afternoon. On second down he takes a pitch from Theismann, starts into the right side of the line behind a pulling guard, then jumps to the outside. Harris comes up to corral him, but Riggins bounces right off him, turns the corner, and skips into the clear. Running down the sideline with Dallas defenders trailing hopelessly, Riggins makes it all the way to the end zone. His brilliant sixty-six-yard dash completes one of the most remarkable psychological comebacks you'll ever see. It's a rare team that blows a 17-point lead, then has the ability and the guts to come back. The crowd is in shock as Moseley makes the score Washington 34, Dallas 21, with 6:54 left to play.

In theory there's time enough for Dallas to put on a closing charge, but the practical question is their will to win—after all, remember that the Cowboys are in the playoffs whatever the outcome today. Springs returns the kickoff to the 20. On first down Staubach tries a screen pass to him, but right linebacker Pete Wysocki reads the play and bursts past the interference to pin Springs for a loss of six. Roger's pass for Hill is broken up by cornerback Joe Lavender. And on third down, from the shot-gun, Staubach is dropped for a loss of five. A smattering of boos can be heard as the offensive unit departs, taking all reasonable hope of victory with them. Standing in his end zone, with the scrimmage line the 9, White punts to Bobby Hammond, who signals a fair catch at the Dallas 48. The clock shows 5:21. If the Skins can pick up a first down or two on the ground, we can head for the exits.

Riggins cracks the right side again, for five yards to the 43.

Then, changing up, the big fullback tries the left side—and fumbles! Luckily for Washington, though, guard Ron Saul recovers for a gain of one. On third and four, with the Dallas defenders stacked up for the run, the give is to Clarence Harmon. He rams up the middle, where he is hit by Harris—and fumbles too! The Cowboys' Randy White, who had been blocked off the play and is lying on the ground, sees the ball rolling to him and grabs it. Dallas will go on offense, with 3:49 to play.

Just as you could forget about Washington throwing a pass in that last series, you can now forget about Dallas running the ball. On every down, Staubach will pass from the shotgun. On first down from his own 41, working against a nickel defense, Roger hits Butch Johnson for fourteen. Next he finds Hill for nineteen. And after that, from the 26, he connects with Springs: The rookie catches the pass at the 8 amid three defenders and, with his back to the end zone, muscles backward and finally squirts over the goal line. Incredible! In three plays that consumed fifty-nine yards, Staubach has brought his club to within striking distance at 34–28.

Now Landry is faced with another critical choice: to kick off deep and trust that the defense will hold Washington without a first down; or to attempt an onside kick that might place the offense in scoring position immediately. Landry puts the task to his defense. Septien's kick sails high but not deep, to the 11. Hammond returns the ball to the 25 with 2:14 to play.

In a real shocker, Theismann opens up with a pass to Danny Buggs, who has beaten cornerback Aaron Kyle. *Buggs drops it.* Hearts are fluttering at the Dallas sideline over that one. On second down Theismann hands to Riggins, his meal ticket, for eight yards off the very productive right side of the line. Third and two coming up, after the two-minute warning. Consider that the pass incompletion on first down meant that Washington used up only fourteen seconds for two plays, without forcing Dallas to use a timeout.

In the Cowboys' final drive of the first half, Staubach fired to Tony Hill for three first-down completions. If the Cowboys are to come on strong in the final minutes of the game, the star receiver from Stanford will have to come up big again.

You know what play is coming: Riggins off the right side. So do the Cowboys. They've known it was coming in the past, too, but Larry Cole and John Dutton haven't been able to do much about it. This time Cole, in his twelfth year with Dallas, shucks off a blocker, grabs Riggins, and takes him down for a loss of two. What a big play! Dallas calls time out with 1:53 on the clock. Mike Bragg, for whom this has not been one of his better days, comes through in the clutch with a forty-four-yard cannonball. Steve Wilson makes the fair catch at the Dallas 25.

The Cowboy offense sets to work. On first down Staubach, in the shotgun, passes over the middle to Hill for twenty. The Washington linebackers blitzed on the play, but were picked up; the Washington backs were playing off the receivers, willing to allow a completion but not the home-run ball. From the 45, the first-down pass is incomplete. The next pass is to Preston Pearson, covered by rookie Ray Waddy, the nickel back. The kid proves easy pickings for the wily graybeard, who makes the catch at the Redskin 33. Timeout, with 1:07 left.

Now Staubach goes to Hill, covered by Waddy in the end zone. Incomplete. Back to Pearson, this time being covered by rookie linebacker Coleman. Preston beats him for a twenty-five-yard completion to the 8! The place is going wild.

Forty-five seconds remain. Staubach looks for Hill in the right corner of the end zone, but Waddy breaks it up. Now Staubach lines up under the center, in conventional T style; on the previous play, operating this close to the goal line, the shotgun had thrown off his timing. Roger fades, looking to throw to his tight end. But the Skins are blitzing, which means that Hill, the secondary receiver, is being covered one-on-one by Parrish. Hill gives a head-and-shoulders fake to the middle, then breaks to the right corner of the end zone again. The pass is lobbed over Parrish, and Hill makes the over-the-shoulder catch. Touchdown!

The game is tied 34–34. The outcome now depends on the extra point. All season long, Septien has missed only one, and he's not about to miss now. The kick is good—Dallas 35, Washington 34, with thirty-nine seconds left. Dallas has reclaimed the momentum, and the lead. But have they won? If there was ever a game to prove that you can't count unhatched chickens, this is it.

Hammond takes Septien's kickoff at the goal line and brings it back to the 26. In a strange call on first down, Theismann throws a screen—a slow-developing, time-consuming play—out to Harmon in the left flat. The pass is complete, but linebacker Mike Hegman upsets Harmon for a one-yard loss. Worse than that, guard Jeff Williams was caught holding; Washington is pushed back to its 16. On first and twenty, Theismann is crunched by Harvey Martin just as he releases the ball; it falls incomplete. Next, Joe is chased out of the pocket by Martin and underthrows his tight end, Don Warren. It is now third down and twenty, with 0:16 to play, a most unpromising position to be in.

Theismann drops back and heaves a bomb to Warren, who is covered by Dallas's nickel back, Aaron Mitchell. Warren has a step on Mitchell, but the pass is a mite underthrown: If Mitchell were to turn around, he might intercept it; instead, he is called for interfering with the receiver!

The penalty is enormous, moving Washington forward thirty-three yards, to its own 49. There are nine seconds left, and one more completion could move the ball within range for a Mark Moseley field goal. The kick would be long, of course, but not impossible—Moseley may have the most powerful leg in football today.

Theismann tries a pass to McDaniel, who is well covered by Kyle. The ball drops incomplete. Five seconds to play. The pass goes over the middle to Warren, who makes his first catch of the day and is downed at the Dallas 42. Theismann runs forward to the game official to call a timeout; the official grants it, with one second left. Moseley and the kicking team can come on for a fifty-nine-yard field-goal attempt. But wait—here comes the man with the gun. "Too late," he says. The game is over!

The Cowboys and their fans are deliriously happy. The Redskins linger on the field, brooding on how they were jobbed by the hometown boys.

Washington, of course, misses the playoffs while Chicago gets in. But the Bears will lose their first-round game, which will not be remembered in pro-football history. And the Cowboys will lose too; that game will not be recalled either, except for being Roger Staubach's last game. He will retire during the off-season, to the immense relief of every defensive back in the NFL. But this roller-coaster game *will* be remembered, and will take on added stature through the years, each time its story is retold. It was a great game among great games.

SCORING

REDSKINS	10	7	0	17 — 34
COWBOYS	0	14	7	14 — 35

Wash.: Moseley, FG, 24.
Wash.: Theismann, 1, run (Moseley, kick).
Wash.: Malone, 55, pass from Theismann (Moseley, kick).
Dal.: Springs, 1, run (Septien, kick).
Dal.: P. Pearson, 26, pass from Staubach (Septien, kick).
Dal.: Newhouse, 2, run (Septien, kick).
Wash.: Moseley, FG, 24.
Wash.: Riggins, 1, run (Moseley, kick).
Wash.: Riggins, 66, run (Moseley, kick).
Dal.: Springs, 26, pass from Staubach (Septien, kick).
Dal.: Hill, 8, pass from Staubach (Septien, kick).

TEAM STATISTICS

	Redskins	Cowboys
First downs	21	27
Rushing yardage	206	110
Passing yardage	167	324
Punt return yardage	0	10
Passes	12-23	24-42
Interceptions by	1	0
Punts	5-38	5-42
Fumbles lost	1	2
Yards penalized	43	74

INDIVIDUAL STATISTICS

RUSHES—Wash.: Riggins, 22 for 151 yards; Malone, 7 for 20; Theismann, 5 for 16; Harmon, 3 for 10; Forte, 2 for 9. Dal.: Springs, 21 for 75; Newhouse, 9 for 22; Johnson, 1 for 13; Staubach, 1 for 0.

PASSES—Wash.: Theismann, 12 of 23 for 200 yards. Dal.: Staubach, 24 of 42 for 336.

RECEPTIONS—Wash.: Buggs, 2 for 49 yards; Harmon, 2 for 31; McDaniel, 2 for 19; Thompson, 2 for 19; Malone, 1 for 55; Forte, 1 for 14; Warren, 1 for 9; Hammond, 1 for 4. Dal.: Hill, 8 for 113; Springs, 6 for 58; P. Pearson, 5 for 108; D. Pearson, 1 for 20; Johnson, 1 for 14; Saldi, 1 for 14; DuPree, 1 for 5; Laidlaw, 1 for 4.

AFTERWORD

That 1979 game brings us up almost to the present day. Will another game come along to squeeze its way onto the Ten Greatest list? Certainly—that's what happened in 1979, in 1974, in 1970. . . . Though that next great football game may not come this year, or the next, or the one after that, it *will* come, and one of our ten great games will be displaced from the list.

Which one will be the first to drop off? Which was the very best game of all? It really is unfair to appraise games played under such differing conditions over nearly a fifty-year span. But it's fun, so let's each arrive at a ranking of the ten games we've seen together. Why don't you do yours first so we can compare, and perhaps argue a bit? I'll offer mine on the next page.

If you'd like to tell me why your list makes more sense, or if I've left off altogether a game *you* feel belongs among the ten greatest ever played, I'd be happy to hear from you: Write to me in care of the publisher: Four Winds Press, 50 West 44th Street, New York, New York 10036.

My ten greatest games, in order of merit:

1. December 24, 1950—Browns 30, Rams 28.
2. December 31, 1967—Packers 21, Cowboys 17.
3. December 28, 1958—Colts 23, Giants 17.
4. December 17, 1933—Bears 23, Giants 21.
5. December 16, 1979—Cowboys 35, Redskins 34.
6. January 1, 1967—Packers 34, Cowboys 27.
7. January 12, 1969—Jets 16, Colts 7.
8. November 8, 1970—Saints 19, Lions 17.
9. December 26, 1965—Packers 13, Colts 10.
10. December 21, 1974—Raiders 28, Dolphins 26.

And, for argument's sake, here are five more games which many people might have placed on their lists:

December 9, 1934—Giants 30, Bears 13; N.Y. scores 27 points in the final quarter, wearing sneakers on the frozen turf.

December 8, 1940—Bears 73, Redskins 0; Chicago demolishes the team that beat them 7–3 three weeks earlier, and its awesome T formation shapes pro football for decades to come.

December 22, 1957—Lions 31, 49ers 27; Detroit roars back from a 27–7 deficit in the second half to win the conference playoff and enter the championship game.

December 24, 1972—Steelers 13, Raiders 7; Pittsburgh achieves its first playoff victory ever on Franco Harris's sixty-yard "immaculate reception" with five seconds to play.

December 24, 1972—Cowboys 30, 49ers 28; Staubach throws two touchdown passes in the final two minutes after coming off the bench to relieve Craig Morton.

These were all great contests, as you can tell from even a one-sentence description—yet I believe that together we have seen ten that were even better. I hope you've enjoyed them.

INDEX

Page numbers in *italics* indicate illustrations.

203